01$1500$1350

Design
with
type

Superficie 290, 1959, by GIUSEPPE CAPOGROSSI, *Rome.*

DESIGN WITH TYPE

by Carl Dair

UNIVERSITY OF TORONTO PRESS

©UNIVERSITY OF TORONTO PRESS 1967
TORONTO AND BUFFALO
REPRINTED 1969, 1974, 1977
PRINTED IN THE UNITED STATES OF AMERICA

AN EARLIER VERSION CONTAINING
PART OF THE MATERIAL IN THIS BOOK
WAS PUBLISHED IN 1952 BY
PELLEGRINI & CUDAHY, NEW YORK

ISBN 0-8020-1426-7
LC 66-23932

preface

Fourteen years have passed since the first writing of this book. The interval has been marked by an enormous increase of interest on the part of both professional and layman in the use of printing type as an active element of communication. This interest is reflected in the establishment and growth of societies devoted to typography, in the spread of exhibitions and conferences, and finally in the founding in New York in 1962 of the International Center for the Typographic Arts with a world-wide membership. The literature of typography has also been enormously augmented in this period.

The first edition of *Design with Type* has long been out of print. This new edition owes its existence to the persistence of Mr Harold Kurschenska, who prevailed upon me to undertake the work of revision, and urged the University of Toronto Press to assume the responsibility of publication. I acknowledge my debt of gratitude.

For this second edition, several considerations have dictated changes. First among these was the very scholarly and kindly critical review in the influential magazine *Print* (VOL. 7, NO. 5) by Mr M. J. Gladstone. A number of his criticisms have been taken to heart in this edition, and I thank Mr Gladstone for drawing attention to some of my original sins; on other points we remain at bodkins drawn.

The assumption made in the first edition that the reader already knew the basic material of typography was unfair to many students of typography who had never held a composing stick. A new chapter in this edition rectifies that error.

The basic principles of design outlined in the original edition remain unchanged, and reappear here. Much of the specimen material which accompanied that original outline quickly became dated. It has therefore been eliminated in this edition. In its stead, I have preferred to use examples of historical importance from both the classic and the contemporary scene.

New influences have created great changes in typography in the decade between editions, and I, along with my colleagues, have been aware of them and have responded to them. It was necessary, therefore, to add new material attempting to assess these influences and their effects, and to try to anticipate what may influence us in the years ahead.

I owe much to many designers and typographers who helped in supplying specimen material; all of them are acknowledged with credit lines. My thanks to each is implicit in the credit.

Because of the special nature of their contributions, I must acknowledge here my thanks to Messrs W. J. H. B. Sandberg, Holland; Diter Rot, Iceland; Massin, France; Oldřich Hlavsa, Czechoslovakia; Victor Vasarely, France; and Giuseppe Capogrossi, Italy. A special acknowledgment to Mr Vasarely is in order: I am so convinced that his paintings challenge the typographer to explore movement on the surface that I have unashamedly accepted his influence in the design of the cover.

To Miss Francess Halpenny of the University of Toronto Press I am deeply indebted for her patience and thoroughness in editing the manuscript and helping me to express my ideas in English prose of greater clarity.

I repeat my original recognition of the influence of the work and writings of Messrs Moholy-Nagy, Mondrian, Kepes, Koffka, and Köhler. To these I must now add the personal influence of Messrs S. L. Hartz, Jan van Krimpen, Jan Tschichold, Maximilien Vox, and Hermann Zapf, and Professors Kapr, Schiller, Weidemann, and Wolter. Each in his own way has had an important part in moulding my thinking and my work.

Toronto, Canada 1966   C.D.

To the memory of

LOUIS BLAKE DUFF

a bibliophile of great knowledge & fine taste

who nurtured my interest in typography

at an early age

& never turned his head away from me

except when I was swiping type

from the hellbox in his printing office

in Welland, Ontario

contents

Have you noticed how picturesque the letter Y is and how innumerable its meanings are? The tree is a Y, the junction of two roads forms a Y, two converging rivers, a donkey's head and that of an ox, the glass with its stem, the lily on its stalk, and the beggar lifting his arms are a Y. This observation can be extended to everything that constitutes the elements of the various letters devised by man. Whatever there is in the demotic language, has been instilled into it by the hieratic language. Hiero glyphics are the root of letters. All characters were originally signs and all signs were once images. Human society, the world, man in his entirety is in the alphabet. Masonry, astronomy, philosophy, all the sciences start here, imperceptible but real, and it must be so. The alphabet is a source . . .

A is a roof with its rafters and traverse-beam, the arch, or it is like two friends who embrace and shake hands

B is the back and the hump

D is a D on a D, that is a 'double-back'—

C is the crescent, is the moon

E is the foundation the pillar and the roof— all architecture contained in a single letter

F is the gallows, the fork

G is the horn

H is the facade of a building with its two towers

I is the war-machine that throws projectiles

J is the plough, the horn of plenty

K signifies one of the basic laws of geometry: the angle of reflection is equal to the angle of incidence

L is the mountain, or the camp within its tents

M is the leg and the foot

N is the door, closed with a cross-bar

O is the sun

P is the porter carrying a burden

Q is the croup and the tail

R signifies rest, the porter leaning on his stick

S is the snake

T is the hammer

U is the urn

V is the vase (that is why U and V are often confused)

X signifies crossed swords, combat —who will be the victor? Nobody knows —that is why philosophers used X to signify fate, and the mathematicians took it for the unknown

Z is the lightning —is God

Y I have already said what Y signifies

So, first comes the house of man, and its construction, then the human body, its build and deformities; then justice, music, the church; war, harvest, geometry; the mountain, nomadic life and secluded life, astronomy, toil and rest; the horse and the snake; the hammer and the urn which— turned over and struck—makes a bell; trees, rivers, roads; and finally destiny and God. That is what the alphabet signifies. —Victor Hugo

? :
was
this
the
beginning

over
10,000
years ago,
during
the ice age,
a man
painted
these spots
and lines
on the wall
of a cave

his meaning
is lost in time,
but his sense
of design
makes this primitive man kin to the graphic designer today

beginnings

The use of written or printed symbols as a basic element of design is not a discovery of our era; it is not even a result of the invention of movable type by Gutenberg. It reaches back into the dawn of civilization, to wherever and whenever man took up a tool and attempted to inscribe on a receptive surface a message to be preserved. It would seem that there was something of an instinctive urge in the dark recesses of the pre-civilized mind towards an orderliness and a pattern in the grouping of the symbols which were to convey this message.

As far back in the history of man's effort to write as you care to go, this innate sense of orderliness has dominated his graphic art. The clay tablets of Mesopotamia and the hieroglyphs of Egypt, the circular tablets of Crete and the precise geometry of the Greek letters, the careful alignment of the flowing characters of the Chinese and the musical lilt of Persian script, the solemnity of the Roman inscriptions and the decorated pages of the Book of Kells – need one go on? – all these attest the desire of the hand that recorded to please the eye that would read. The forms of these patterns were many, and they arose out of the whole composite of the art and the culture from which they stemmed.

The invention of movable type did not change this urge towards the beautiful in graphic presentation; it simply provided the means, denied to the ancients, of reproducing the original work and so widening the public who would see and read. The early printers of Mainz and Basle and Venice were not indifferent to the obligation this freedom imposed on them, and so they sought, with meticulous care and craftsmanship, to make

The Phaistos disc, dating to approximately 1700 B.C., was found in Crete, and is the earliest example of a terra cotta tablet in which separate stamps – the precursor of movable type – have been 'printed' into the clay. Note the organization into a spiral.

each letter, each line, each page as beautiful as they had been in the manuscripts which had sired the art of printing. The type cutter put all his skill and sense of form into the creation of beautiful individual letters; the typesetter sought to combine these characters into pages of dignity; and the pressman took painstaking care to reproduce the whole uniformly, with just the right amount of ink, so that none of this elegance might escape making its timeless imprint upon paper.

Each in his own time, often with crude tools poised against resisting surfaces, tried to make the written record the epitome of the art and culture of his own period. Bone against clay, chisel against stone, brush against silk, quill against parchment, lead against paper, each tool made its characteristic mark, and each surface received the impression in its characteristic way. The hand of the artist accepted his materials and made the most of them. The tradition is long and the urge is deep.

The speed of reproduction of the written word by machines in a modern printing plant would astound the ancients. But if they could see it, they might wonder why, with the labour of writing so eased by mechanical devices, we are not able to put even greater thought into the design of our printing.

No doubt these same ancients would also not understand the cost sheet we would show them; they would find the urgency of deadlines as an excuse for shoddiness incomprehensible; they would be bewildered by the complex relationships of individual specialists involved in doing the work they once did single-handed. And they would probably return to their primitive tools shaking their heads with awe at the accomplishments of twentieth-century printing technology, but yet distressed that all the art and loving care that they had lavished on the written and printed word counted for so little. They might well conclude that, while we can produce more and faster, they could give a better product.

Taking a moment for sober reflection, and looking at the

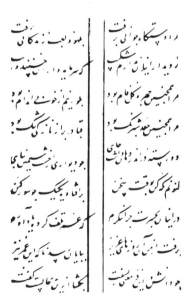

Four classic examples of richly organized and textured records: top left, the Egyptian Book of the Dead; *top right, a Chinese epitaph from the Chin dynasty (3rd century B.C.); lower left, a fifth-century manuscript in Rustic capitals; above, a Persian manuscript.*

CVSPIVM · AED

heritage of beauty and craftsmanship they have left for us, we must concede that perhaps they are right. Somewhere along the line the tradition has faltered; at some indefinable point along the road the aesthetic urge has been submerged; and to day, at the pinnacle of technical ability to reproduce the printed word, we have fallen short of the high artistic standards that our predecessors with more primitive equipment set for us.

The dual drive of economy and speed has led the printer since the nineteenth century to abrogate his rôle as a designer. Dazzléd by the introduction and constant improvement of powered typesetting machines and printing presses, he became so oriented to the cost sheet and the production chart that the basic object of printing – communicating through the printed word – became a secondary consideration, if it was considered at all. Investment in the machinery of reproduction in the press room rose, while investment in the means of preparing the thing to be reproduced fell. Type faces became worn and obso lete. Composing room craftsmen were put under time-motion studies which ruled out a creative approach to their craft and measured their craftsmanship by time rather than the appear ance of the product. It was inevitable that some printing plants should eliminate the composing room entirely and devote themselves to quantity production only. All that was left for the printer to offer was faster delivery, a lower price, or both.

This decline in printing as an art had its parallel in all branches of the industrial world, and the only revolt against increasing cheapness as an end in itself came from a few un regenerate hand craftsmen who still lovingly shaped wood and metal and fabrics – and found a market among those of taste who could enjoy a fine piece of workmanship and could afford to pay for it. In the printing world, it was the private press movement and a few idealistic printing houses that kept the flickering flame of craftsmanship from being snuffed out by the headwind of industrialization.

Price competition, however, is a vicious downward spiral that dooms itself; greater and greater capital investments were required for newer and faster machines that would produce cheaper and cheaper printed matter. As in the case of other industries, some printers finally turned to design as a means of lifting themselves above the competition and, by offering a far better and more effective product, sought to get a better price. Perhaps, they reasoned, the business executive who will pay more for a hand-tailored suit designed and fitted to his individual physical form would pay more for a printing job custom-made for his corporate needs.

The design-oriented craftsman who used to stick type at the case bought himself a drawingboard and a new suit, and became a graphic designer – like his industrial counterpart, a kind of aristocrat of his industry. Good design, it was discovered, was good business.

But the designer was now outside his industry; he learned its technology only as a means to an end. As a result, design today tends toward personal exhibitionism, often technically impractical and unsuited to its purpose. The excitement of discovery of the wealth of effects that can be gained through simple letterforms can sometimes obscure the intention of communication. In the development of a new design approach, visual stimulation and effective communication will move more closely together until they merge in common design objectives.

The end product may not look like a Roman inscription or a Gutenberg page, but it will be the result of the honest use of tools and materials at the service of creative printing to meet the needs of our times.

Two handsome manuscripts above, the seventh-century Book of Kells, and below, a page of Carolingian minuscules, written in the court of Charlemagne in a letter standardized by Alcuin of York.

the nature of type

Good design in any field demands that the designer know the materials with which he is working. It is an unfortunate product of today's industrial methods that the man who knows typographic material most intimately because he 'sticks' type day after day is no longer the designer of printing, and that, on the other hand, the designer is usually a man who knows his material only at second hand, and could not execute, by himself, the work which he plans.

The information which follows is no substitute for the actual 'feel' of type; the best this account can hope to do is to supply an elementary knowledge of printing types and how they are handled. Thus the errors of ignorance may be avoided, though the sure touch that comes from working intimately with type may be harder to acquire.

For an understanding of the physical nature of type it is best to go back to the invention of the printing process, generally attributed to Johann Gutenberg of Mainz, in the years between 1440 and his completion of the first printed Bible around 1456.

The principle of applying ink to a relief surface and transferring the relief pattern to a sheet of paper in a press had been known long before, both in Europe and in the Orient. But the relief surface had always been a completely engraved page on a single block of wood – illustration and text together. Gutenberg's great contribution was in devising a method whereby individual letters could be shaped once, and then cast in unlimited quantities for assembly, disassembly, and reassembly: the invention of movable type.

This was a considerable technical achievement, much in

2

advance of its time. Of the invention the *Encyclopædia Britan*nica says: 'In the light of our own mass-production society, we can recognize in the invention of printing the first example of our own manufacturing techniques: standardized mass production by means of assembling interchangeable parts designed and manufactured for precision fit. Detroit was anticipated in Mainz about 1450. Gutenberg was certainly the first modern industrial genius.' He was, of course, in a wider view, much more than that: his invention made possible the wider dissemination of information and thought, and later mass literacy and higher levels of education for more people.

We do not know today exactly how, or if, Gutenberg cast metal types, but certainly within a few years after his printing of the Bible, his erstwhile partner, Peter Schoeffer, was cutting master letters in a hard metal, probably steel, and driving each into a softer metal, such as brass or copper, to make a matrix – a sunken impression of the letter in the metal.

What we do believe Gutenberg invented was the adjustable mould. It must in essence have been two L's of metal. When these two pieces were slid together the mould would maintain a precisely uniform height, but it could be changed in width to accommodate letters varying from the narrow 'I' to the wide 'M'. The matrix of the letter was put in position at the bottom of the opening of the mould, and the mould was adjusted to the exact width of the letter; then it was possible to pour into the mould molten lead which, when hard, could be removed as a long shank of metal with an exact raised reproduction of the original letter on one end.

This is printing type.

Five hundred years later, we are still following these methods for almost all of our printed matter. Machines have been introduced to speed up the casting of type and its assembly into pages of text, but the fundamental principle of pouring or forcing molten lead into a mould against a matrix of a letter is

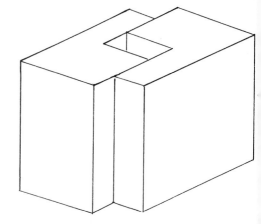

A diagram of the probable (though by no means certain) shape of the adjustable mould which we believe Gutenberg may have invented.

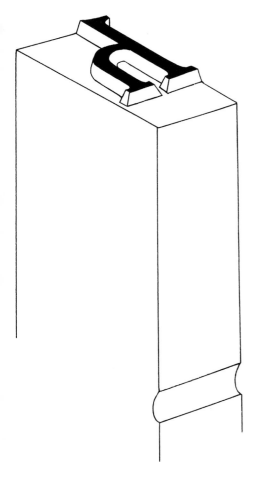

still the basis for almost all of the printing which is done in the world today. The use of film negatives to replace the matrix and mould in typesetting machines has been introduced recently, and will become increasingly important. It has not at this time seriously challenged the supremacy of 'hot metal' methods of casting type.

Once the technical problems of casting individual types had been solved, printing spread rapidly during the fifteenth century. By the year 1500, a bare forty-five years after the completion of Gutenberg's Bible, there were 150 printing plants in the city of Venice alone.

But the technical achievement was only the first part of the business of printing; before a printer could print books, he had either to be an artist or to secure the services of an artist who could design and engrave an alphabet. In the infancy of printing, every printer had his own types cut for him individually; the kind of letters he used was the sure trade-mark of his work. Only in the sixteenth century did typefounding become a separate business which supplied printers with types cast from the same matrices.

Throughout the history of printing, the design of letter forms has challenged artists, until today our repertoire of type faces numbers well over five thousand. Yet many of the letters which were designed for printers in the first fifty years of printing are the models for the finest types we use today; the type in which the text of this book is set is a faithful rendering of a letter which was first used in 1495.

A complete set of characters for any one size of any type face is called a 'fount' or 'font', and will consist of ROMAN CAPITALS, roman lower case (small letters), SMALL CAPITALS (which are the same height as the lower-case letters), *ITALIC CAPITALS* and *italic lower case*, a full set of punctuation marks in roman and italic, and usually two types of figures, those which align with the capitals and with each other, called

ABCDEFGHIJKLMNOPQRSTUVW
XYZ1234567890$&?!.,:;-()"[]¶§†‡abcd
efghijklmnopqrstuvwxyz1234567890fiflff
ffiffl *ABCDEFGHIJKLMNOPQRSTU*
VWXYZ1234567890$&?!.,:;-()"[]¶§†‡
abcdefghijklmnopqrstuvwxyz1234567890fi
flfffiffl ABCDEFGHIJKLMNOPQRSTUVWX
YZ *ABCDEFGHIJKLMNOPQRSTUVWXYZ*

'lining' figures, and those which match the lower-case letters and are called 'old style' or 'non-ranging' figures.

For every face of type there is a particular relationship be_l tween the height of the full ascending and descending letters and the normal lower-case letter. The height of the latter is referred to as the 'x-height' – for the simple reason that the lower-case letter 'x' is the only one which has four flat terminals resting exactly at the base and at the upper line of the lower-case height. How greatly the x-height of types can vary, and the effect this variation has on the optical size of type, can be seen in the following setting:

These two paragraphs are set in types of the same size, though one appears much larger than the other. The difference between the two lies in the greater x-height and the consequent shortening of ascenders and descenders in the type used in the second setting compared to the type used in the first.

These two paragraphs are set in types of the same size, though one appears much larger than the other. The difference between the two lies in the greater x-height and the consequent shortening of ascenders and descenders in the type used in the second setting

Why are they then referred to as being the same size? Because the depth of the metal shanks on which the letters of the two types are cast is the same. They differ optically because the x-height is a larger or smaller proportion of the depth of the metal face.

Type sizes are measured in units called 'points', a system of measurement used exclusively in typography. The typographic point is approximately 1/72 of an inch. Thus a type of 72-point size will have a body almost exactly one inch from the top of

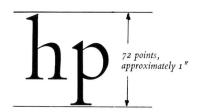

72 points,
approximately 1"

This is 6-pt. type
This is 8-pt. type
This is 10-pt. type
This is 12-pt.type
This is 14-pt. type
This is 18-pt. type
This is 24-pt. type
This is 30-pt. type
s is 36-pt. type
s 42-pt. type
48-pt. type
60-pt. ty
72-pt.t

the 'h' to the bottom of the 'p'. Most types are cast in the sizes shown in the accompanying chart, and some types are cast in intermediate sizes of 7-, 9-, and 11-point body sizes. Occa sionally 16-pt., 20-pt., 28-pt., and 54-pt. types are cast.

While type sizes are referred to by the basic unit of measure ment, the point, linear measurements in typography are re ferred to in 'picas'. A pica bears the same relationship to a point that a foot bears to an inch: a pica consists of 12 points. When referring to the length of a line, we speak of it as so many picas wide; a block of copy is so many picas in depth. There are approximately 6 picas to the inch.

These are the basic measurements of typography, but two others should be mentioned. Newspapers use an otherwise obsolete measurement known as the 'agate line'. Originally this was the name of a size of small type, in which all advertise ments once were set. Newspaper space is sold in units which are one column wide and one agate line in depth, with four teen lines making up one inch in depth.

Secondly, there is a square measurement in typography (all the above have been linear measurements). This is the 'em', and it is used as the basis for charging for typesetting. The em is not a standard size, but rather it is the square of the size of type being used. An em of 8-point type is eight points square, of 10-point type, ten points square. Thus, if a line of 8-point type is being set 20 picas long, it will contain 30 ems of type (20 picas equals 20 × 12 equals 240 points; 240 points divided by 8 equals 30).

A given text, like this page, when set in type contains not only letters, but spaces where there is no printing at all – such as those between words. These spaces are measured in the square measure – ems and fractions of ems. A full square is called an em (or 'mut') quad; a space which is half of the square is called an en (or 'nut') quad. The next smaller space is called a 'thick space' or a 3-to-em space, and it is one-third of an em in width. Similarly there are 4-to-em, 5-to-em, and 6-to-em spaces.

The lines set below will indicate what happens to a line of type when each of these spaces is used; the black mark at the beginning of the line is the actual size of the space.

This line is spaced with em quads
This line is spaced with en quads
This line is spaced with 3-to-em spaces
This line is spaced with 4-to-em spaces
This line is spaced with 5-to-em spaces
This line is spaced with 6-to-em spaces

Spacing can also occur between the lines of type to increase the white channel between the lines. The materials used are strips of lead which are 1 point, 1½ points, 2 points, 3 points, or 4 points in thickness; these are called 'leads'. Strips of 6-point or 12-point thickness are called 'slugs'. The purpose of introducing leads between the lines is to help readability where lines are so long that the eye, in moving back to pick up the beginning of a new line, tends to 'double' – to pick up the line already read. The leads, by increasing the white space between the lines, help to guide the eye back to the beginning of the next line.

The amount of white which already exists between the lines because of the ascenders and descenders will vary, of course, with the x-height of the face of type being used. The two type faces we have already used in examining x-height will demonstrate. Look at the difference in the amount of white normally existing between the lines without the use of leads in the examples on the next two pages. Then examine what happens when a few lines of text of each of these types are leaded.

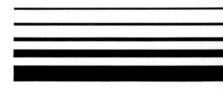

The thicknesses of leads, from the top down: 1 pt., 1½ pt., 2 pt., 3 pt., 6 pt., and 12 pt.

This paragraph has no leading

Typography today is the art of visual communication, an art which has for its materials ink, paper, and twenty-six abstract symbols. The methods of using these materials to gain the maximum of legibility constitute the science of typography.

This paragraph has a 1-point lead between the lines

Typography today is the art of visual communication, an art which has for its materials ink, paper, and twenty-six abstract symbols. The methods of using these materials to gain the maximum of legibility constitute the science of typography.

This paragraph has a 2-point lead between the lines

Typography today is the art of visual communication, an art which has for its materials ink, paper, and twenty-six abstract symbols. The methods of using these materials to gain the maximum of legibility constitute the science of typography.

This paragraph has a 3-point lead between the lines

Typography today is the art of visual communication, an art which has for its materials ink, paper, and twenty-six abstract symbols. The methods of using these materials to gain the maximum of legibility constitute the science of typography.

Obviously type faces which have a large x-height need more leading than those with a small x-height. So it is hard to generalize as to when leading becomes necessary for easy reading. A general rule would be that two and a half alphabets, i.e., 65 characters, is the maximum length of line that can be read without leading in the case of type with a small x-height; but the maximum becomes two alphabets (52 characters) for a letter with a large x-height. However, leading between the lines will always improve the horizontal flow of reading, even

Typography today is the art of visual communication, an art which has for its materials
ink, paper, and twenty-six abstract symbols.
The methods of using these materials to gain
the maximum of legibility constitute the science

This paragraph has no leading

Typography today is the art of visual communication, an art which has for its materials
ink, paper, and twenty-six abstract symbols.
The methods of using these materials to gain
the maximum of legibility constitute the science

This paragraph has a 1-point lead between the lines

Typography today is the art of visual communication, an art which has for its materials
ink, paper, and twenty-six abstract symbols.
The methods of using these materials to gain
the maximum of legibility constitute the science

This paragraph has a 2-point lead between the lines

Typography today is the art of visual communication, an art which has for its materials
ink, paper, and twenty-six abstract symbols.
The methods of using these materials to gain
the maximum of legibility constitute the science

This paragraph has a 3-point lead between the lines

with lines shorter than the maximums indicated above.

These then, are the bricks and mortar of the typographic art:
metal types, spaces, leads and slugs, and the system of measure
ment employed. This over-simplified summary of the materi
als of typography is for the benefit of the student and the
uninitiated; it should not be construed as a substitute for the
years of training and the knowledge of a multitude of details
which the skilled compositor has acquired, and the familiarity
with his material that such experience brings.

The basic element of typography is the individual character –
letter, numeral, or punctuation mark.

The matter does not end there – it starts there. Without a
fundamental and deep appreciation of the form of individual
letters, no designer can be effective, any more than a bricklayer
who does not know the heft of an individual brick can build
a wall. Typography starts with the letter and builds from there;
it is the basic unit of all printed communication.

Most typesetters and graphic designers have an innate appreciation of a letter's structure; they are sensitive to the well-
drawn curve, the subtle proportions, the grace of line which

ALDO NOVARESE, *type designer for Società Nebiolo in
Turin, offers this diagram of the relationship between
letters and the architecture of different periods.*

characterize a favourite type face. It is a standing testimonial to
the basically good taste of printing houses that type faces which
lack good form do not have a long life. Typographic specimen
books are literally strewn with these casualties. Many an alphabetic abortion has been unceremoniously dumped into the
printer's hellbox after the initial novelty has worn off and the
shallowness of the design has become apparent.

If an appreciation of the individual letter is the beginning of
typographic design, an ability to make the most of the single
character is the fulfilment of it. And here is where the analogy
of the bricklayer breaks down; for he can only lay bricks one
beside the other, one row on top of the other, in a monotonous
repetition of his basic unit. Once in a while his creative urges
will get the better of him and he will try to break that monotony by introducing brick of another colour in a patterned
formation – the creative urge can never be entirely stifled. But
the printer fares a little better; he has more scope for creative

imagination. He can, of course, lay letters one beside the other, one row below the other, and create a pleasant but monotonous sort of brick-wall typography. But he doesn't have to do this, since his basic unit is available in many different sizes, shapes, and weights, and the open space can flow around and through his units in a manner that would be hazardous in bricklaying.

Just examine the montage of different characters illustrated here, each of them readily recognizable as a letter 'a'. These are culled from only a few of the multitude of type faces which are available today. Some of these individual characters have slight family resemblances to others in the group; but whether the resemblance is slight or great, the fact remains that each character is a personality in its own right, with its own individual appearance and mannerisms; we might even go so far as to invest it with a distinct personality. But while each and every one of these specimens of the letter 'a' is an interesting form in itself, with a special beauty of proportion and line to make it attractive, at the same time each of these letters becomes a more or less anonymous unit when combined with other letters. Then its individual personality is lost in the larger unit, just as a person is an anonymous unit in a crowd.

Standing by itself, a letter can create a focal point in a typographic design; its size, or its unusual characteristics, or the very fact of its isolation can draw attention to it, and thus it will swing the reader into the message. The mediaeval scribes were aware of this basic principle of design and applied it in their use of decorative, coloured initial letters, sometimes even containing a miniature painting. The use of decorative initial letters was continued by the early printers, who often had them coloured by hand, and the initial is still common in bookwork today.

In modern commercial printing, too, the initial letter plays an important rôle, but it has more flexibility, since it is not necessarily regimented into a fixed position by having to be

IN Chrif
noic: ac glo꞉iofc ᵹ
nis: Post ꝙ deo o
arbo꞉é Joþánis
per actionibus:m
auditoꝛibus aliqu
ter in voce declar
Jccirco ego bapti
de facto Blafio ꞇ
ufꝗꞽ iuris docto꞉:
cibus nõnullo꞉um mco꞉ū fcholarū motus:opu
lum quoddaꝫ fuper dicta arbo꞉e actionū: facere
defcribere confꞇitui:de actionibus ꞇ natura cari
nuncupatū. Jn꞊quo omiffis que fcribunꞇ fuper

The creation of decorative initials is the proper pursuit of book designer or printer. ERHARD RATDOLT'S *fifteenth-century initial is shown above, while below is a contemporary design by* FRANK NEWFELD, *Toronto.*

II Corinthians

tanding in Corinth in the m
Where the wild blossoms springing
Contend with marble foliage worn
Which shall exhibit the more ageles

Letters are a lot like people: they come in all shapes and
sizes, with different personalities and charms and foibles,
but all with the same basic reason and purpose
for existence.

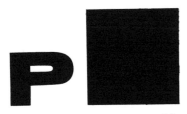

Two variations of the letter a *used as a commercial mark: the first made up from type rules, and the second drawn by* GEORGE TSCHERNY *of New York for the Aluminum Association.*

A simple but strong statement is made by this mark designed for his own use by the Dutch typographer-architect, PIET ZWART, *whose last name means 'black'.*

Three trade marks by FELIX BELTRAN *of Havana: left, mark for the fourth exhibition of editorial art; upper right, for Kapovich Arquitecto; below, for Nacional Importadora.*

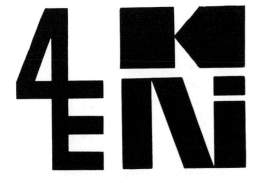

the first letter of a body of text. The freedom accorded the commercial designer allows him not only to determine the position of the initial in relation to the text, but also to select an initial of pleasing form, even a lower-case letter if he desires.

But while the most important function of the individual letter can be its use as a focal point of typographic design, it has many other functions as well. Letters have even acquired symbolic connotations for us; terms such as UN, USA, OK, TV have a world of significance symbolized by letters, to the point where they become spoken words in themselves. A letter, or combination of letters can be, and have been, used to effect striking monograms. The creative printer-designer, alive to his client's need for individual identification, can create from his type cases trade-marks of permanent value. The few examples shown will indicate how readily initials are accepted as identifying marks in the consumer's mind. Calling an individual or a firm by his or its initials is a token of respectful affection, and such tokens have become a part of our daily speech. The designer who is conscious of the forms of letters and symbols will, of course, move beyond the limitations of type letters and employ his ingenuity in combining or modifying letters to create marks of greater distinctiveness.

The individual letter can also, by repetition, become a decorative element in typography. It is very flexible, offering itself as a border, an area of a given shape, or a complete background. The only restriction in the diversity of these applications is the ingenuity of the designer or printer himself; once he begins to explore the possible combinations, they seem to be endless.

Numerals can often serve the same purpose as individual letters; a figure 5 will suggest a perfume, 7 is associated with a soft drink. Numerals are also effective in ticking off selling points in a methodical manner, and become, in themselves, functional and pleasant elements of design.

Even punctuation has its symbolism – the interrogation mark

Monograms by Belgian designer MICHELE OLYFF: *at left, IDF, with the letters turned on side for structural effect; below, CF for a commercial firm, DG for architect Dugardyn, and the designer's own mark.*

A single wood letter fills the page of an advertisement for a firm of printers in Milan. Designed by FRANCO GRIGNANI.

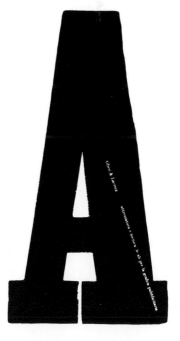

unmistakably represents the question asked; it is the doubt symbolized. The exclamation point, the comma, the paragraph mark, all have immediate significance if given dominant position; and each of them is a design element around which good typography can be built.

Oversize characters run in colour can be dramatic and compelling. Old cases of wood type often yield such large characters, and the compositor with a flair for using rules can often build up letters which can lift an ordinary setting of type into the category of the striking and unusual.

The letter, the number, the single unit of the typographic structure thus has unending possibilities in the hands of the printer or designer who loves it for itself and will make the most of his basic material. And having learned to use this element effectively, by itself, he will also understand more fully how to use it effectively in combination with other letters: in words, in lines, in masses.

Logograms by DITER ROT.

Letters are like molecules when they combine with one an
other; each arrangement of the individual components in com
bination creates an entirely new result. Molecules of hydrogen
and oxygen, for example, can combine with each other, and
with other elements, to make a gas, a liquid, or a solid, each
substance with characteristics all its own, unlike any other sub
stance. In each case, the essential characteristics of the original
elements are completely lost in the new product; when the
gases hydrogen and oxygen are combined in the ratio of two
hydrogen molecules and one oxygen molecule the result is not
a gas, but a liquid – water.

Precisely the same thing happens when letters combine to
form words; the combination is an entirely new form with its
own connotation, divorced from any meanings inherent in any
of the units which comprise it. Here is a simple example, with
two letters which, when their positions are reversed, convey
entirely different meanings:

ah   ha

The individual 'molecules' of the word have lost their signi
ficance, a new form emerges from their combination, and new
meanings are associated with the combination according to the
sequence of the units.

The important point of this argument is that when a word
is created, it takes a typographic form which makes it instantly
recognizable without reference to the phonetic structure sym
bolized by the separate characters which form the word. The
word is the picture of the thing, or the idea – a picture just as

Four letters can be grouped in twenty-four different combinations, but with the letters chosen below, only one combination makes a familiar configuration which we immediately recognize as a word.

epyt	pyte	ypet	tepy
epty	pyet	ypte	tpey
eypt	peyt	yept	tyep
eytp	pety	yetp	teyp
etpy	ptey	ytep	tpye
etyp	ptye	ytpe	type

real as the pictures which constituted primitive writing, even though they have now developed into abstractions.

But this word-picture which is a product of the arrangement of the letters can often be strengthened by the kind of type used to convey it. The type can, by its particular form, emphasize the quality of the meaning of the word, or approximate its sound. The soft sigh, ah, and the explosive burst, ha, might find typographical equivalents thus:

ah　　**ha**

Human beings very readily associate sounds and emotional reactions with graphic forms. The great psychologist, Wolfgang Köhler, experimented with two abstract linear shapes and two meaningless 'words' which subjects were asked to pair off; most people associated the correct pairs without hesitation – the words seemed to describe the forms and the forms seemed to be visual equivalents of the words.

Typographically, then, it is possible to convey the essence of a word through the proper choice of type faces so as to get an emotional response to the word through its associations. Such a highly charged word can become a focal point of the composition in display printing. Of course it is not the printer's task to choose such a word initially – that is the job of the copywriter. But it is the printer's responsibility to be able to single out the interesting word from the typewritten copy for title-page, jacket, or advertisement and recognize that here could be the solution to his typographic problem, the single element around which his whole composition could be built. The ability to read the copy, understand its meaning, and pounce on the key word or phrase for translation into typographic terms: this is what a client has a right to expect from his printing designer. When the material is complex the designer may, of course, confer with his client on matters of interpretation and emphasis.

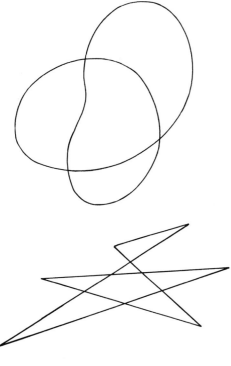

takete　　　maluma

An ability to recognize the appropriate word itself, and to play on the particular letter-forms which are used to make up the word, is the basis for every successful trade name. Many famous brand and company names have relied on the repetition of a given type style, carefully thought out to convey the spirit of the enterprise or product, to create a typographic image, a visual pattern, that becomes identified with the product or firm. Magazines attach particular importance to the type style used for the publication's name; one has only to mention the names of *Life*, *Time*, the *New Yorker*, and so on, and an image of the kind of type used for these words will come to mind automatically.

The word, used as a unit of design, can have many and varied applications in typography from the single word 'menu' on the cover of a bill of fare to the cover of a catalogue where the name of a firm or product dominates. There are as many ways of handling this unit as there are type faces in the printer's composing-room, and there are many different treatments of the single word when properly set. The repetition of the chosen word, set identically, to create an area of colour, to form a border, or to provide an entire background, not only makes an interesting design, but can, of course, also serve to emphasize the message. A repeated word can become a shape when it is set again and again in diminishing sizes.

The word, as a unit with a form of its own, can also have a positive directional value. A composition can acquire a dyna mic quality if, for instance, the word to be stressed is set at a right angle to the conventional horizontal position. Judgment and good taste are called for here, but the single word in a vertical position and in opposition to other horizontal ele ments, can give a strong visual thrust within a given space.

The juggling of type that varies in size, in style, or in both size and style, can be highly effective as an attention-getting device if it is carried through skilfully. The results may even

A jumble of letters can often create an interesting pattern without destroying legibility, as shown above, where the syllables are carefully grouped for identification. Below, a piece of hand-lettering, one of the rare cases when letters have been successfully shaped into an appropriate illustration; designed by WILLIAM IRISH *for a Toronto theatre.*

Joining letters gives individuality to the title of an Italian architectural magazine, above, and meaning to a label design (rejected) below.

The German word for 'cross-section' is handled appropriately by HERMANN OTTO above, while Prague designer JIRÍ RATHOUSKY creates a compact signature for a magazine below.

be criticized as being illegible, but in some instances the strength of the pattern lies in the very fact that it challenges the reader to decipher it. Once the typographical jig-saw puzzle is solved, it will be remembered as a special configuration of letters, readily identified when encountered again.

Elimination of the space between letters can also create a special pattern which, once identified, is not easily forgotten. This compression of the letters can take place laterally, with one letter pressing against its neighbour, or vertically, with the words stacked one above the other.

The eye can often recognize a word even when portions of the letters are missing; it simply fills them in. Words in a typographic design can therefore be cropped at top, bottom, or sides, and still be identified. This ability of the reader to recognize portions of words has been exploited to good effect for small-space advertisements which literally thrust them selves into the adjoining (and unpaid) space.

All of these techniques acquire a new type of impact when the letters are reversed against a black ground. Here the inner forms of the letters become the dominant pattern, and the word is literally recognized by the negative, unprinted word. This subject is discussed at greater length in chapter 14.

Taking the word as the focal point of typographic composi tion is probably the easiest stratagem to employ in capturing and holding attention and interest: it requires that the designer recognize the word, appreciate its significance, explore its pos sibilities, and translate its essential meaning and feeling into type. These devices should never degenerate into mere tricks to capture the wandering eye of the reader; they should be grounded in the essential meanings of the words themselves, so that the special configuration that emerges is meaningful to the reader, so that it is a visual exposition of the idea the words convey. This visual-verbal link as a way of achieving a single connotation demands a creative approach to the word itself.

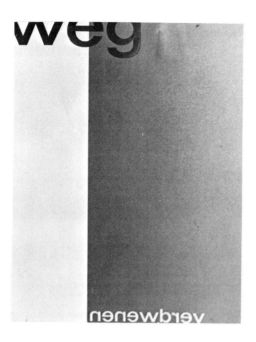

Words set in type can be given the very quality of their meaning: top left, 'The Vanishing Road' designed by WIM CROUWEL, Amsterdam; centre left, TONY PALLADINO of New York gives illustrative value to the type, while below, LADISLAV SUTNAR of New York invests a logotype for a mechanical computer with a mathematical look. At upper right, an expressive cover for a Czech typographic magazine, designed by OLDŘICH HLAVSA of Prague. Below, Draeger, a famous name in French printing, is cropped to a narrow ribbon by its art director, RENÉ TOUTAIN.

TUCKAWAYABUCKADAY

la velocità modifica la grafica
la velocità modifica il colore

la velocità modifica la vv ii ss ii oo nn ee

Just as the letter is a unit which enters into the aggregation we call a word, so words themselves become simple units in the larger relationship of the phrase or sentence. But, unlike letters, the individual words do not lose their identity in this new relationship; visually, they merge as part of the general pattern of the typographic line, but they retain their own pattern and meaning through their separation from other words by space.

It would thus seem that two objectives are in conflict – on the one hand we create a line which is a homogeneous design unit and, on the other hand, we try to satisfy the fundamental requirement of legibility by allowing adequate word separation. There is a subtle point of balance here: what is the precise space which lets in just enough white to make it immediately apparent where one word ends and the next begins, but does not chop up the line into a series of word islands?

There can be no fixed rules for establishing just how much this space should be; it will vary with each type face and with each type size. A type face with a large x-height, as illustrated in the second chapter, will need more space between the words than a type with a small x-height; a wide face will need more than a narrow face. Certainly a type set in a large size needs relatively less space between words than it would set in a very small size, as the examples will indicate.

The words in this line are separated by a 4-to-em space,
and the separation of the words is inadequate for easy reading.

Increasing the space between the words to an en quad
improves the legibility of this small type.

But an en quad is too much for this size.

The words in this line are separated by a 4-to-em space.

Opposite page: on a billboard a simple and direct verbal message for a bank commands attention and gives a sense of urgency when the words are joined. Designed by CLIFF WILTON. *Below, copy designed by* FRANCO GRIGNANI *of Milan emphasizes linear elements and interprets the effect of speed.*

The ideal setting of text would allow the proper amount of space for the style and size of type being used, and would give that space without variation throughout the text. But this is an ideal that can be achieved only if the typesetter is allowed to leave the right-hand edge of the setting uneven, as has been done in this paragraph.

In point of fact, most modern printing, especially book printing, requires that all lines be set to the same length, and a typesetter uses variations in the space between words to extend his line to the full width. So the ideal spacing can rarely be achieved, though a good craftsman will avoid the extremes of excessively wide or excessively narrow spacing.

A typesetter can give more consistently good spacing if the line is long enough to enable him to distribute the space varia tions evenly through a number of word separations. Take an extreme example: a compositor setting on a narrow measure comes to the words 'contemporary philosophical thought' at the beginning of his line. With tight spacing he gets in this much:

contemporary philosophical though

If he puts in the final t, he must remove all the space from the line: obviously not permissible. He cannot divide the word 'thought' with a hyphen. So he must of necessity carry the whole word to the next line, and the space in his first line is excessive:

contemporary   philosophical
thought takes the stand that we are

The experienced typographic designer will avoid confront ing his typesetter with this kind of spacing problem. If the measure *must* be short, he will specify that the right-hand edge may remain unjustified, or 'ragged'. If the type is to be justified right and left, he will make the measure wider so that the average line will contain eight to ten words – or more. It goes without saying that he has examined the manuscript before making his choice; obviously ten words of technical language will make a longer line than ten words of a child's story.

With all of the special conditions outlined above in mind, a general rule of thumb can be established to guide the typographer: in normal text sizes, a 3-to-em space should be the maximum word-space, with latitude allowed to the typesetter to help him deal with special situations where a word cannot be broken. Where a word *can* be broken, it is certainly better to break it at the end of a line than to use excessive spacing to 'drive out' the line.*

Having seen the prime importance of legibility of the line in copy intended to be read and absorbed, we can proceed with our discussion of the line as an element of design in typography.

In considering the design characteristics of the letter and the word we were primarily concerned with a study of their form. A new factor enters into the picture when we reach the line. Called 'texture', it results from the repetition of the dominant design characteristic of each individual letter. Texture is a word which has not had much currency in the printing trade except in respect to paper surfaces; it has been considered an 'arty' term applicable to the surface of old wood, textiles, pottery, rock, and so on. But it is important to see its application to type if good typographic design is to be fully understood.

Typographic textures, like all other textures, can be very subtle or very obvious. To make the point clear, so that we

*The hyphen has always been an unsatisfactory symbol to indicate a word break. It has two faults: it fails to distinguish between a broken word at the end of a line and a compound word; visually, it disrupts the even right-hand edge which is the purpose of justified lines, and becomes particularly objectionable when successive lines end in hyphens. In this book, the author has used a new character (which it is his conceit to call a 'fracture') in the hope that it may eliminate both these objections and gain some following in fine printing.

Texture is best understood when we cannot read the message and therefore do not become involved in meaning. Above, an Arab calligrapher creates a beautiful pattern from a Koranic text. (Courtesy Arab World.) Below, the Cyrillic writing of 'Boris Gudonov' becomes a rich texture on the title page of a recent Russian book.

SELIG SEGAL *of Jerusalem created this massive architectural texture for Israel's Independence Day commemorative coin in 1966. Compare its feeling with the painting by* CAPOGROSSI *facing the title page. It is interesting to remember that Hebrew letters are used for numerals, and Israel's 18th anniversary is represented by Yod and Het, the tenth and eighth letters. An ancient Jewish game involves discovering hidden meaning in words by manipulating the numerical values of their letters. Thus, Yod and Het when transposed spell 'hai', meaning alive. The inscription reads 'The people of Israel live on', with the two characters at the base doubling for the word 'live' and for the numeral 18. (Courtesy Government of Israel.)*

understand exactly what is meant by texture, let us consider an obvious example. The dominant design characteristic of any single character of a script such as Bank Script is the heavy slanted stroke; all the rounded portions of the letters are light and unobtrusive. In a type line of this script the repetition of the strong slanted line of the characters creates a pattern of diagonals throughout the line of type; this pattern is the *texture* of the type. And to emphasize how accurate the word texture is in describing this effect, consider the similarity between this type pattern and the dominant diagonal pattern in a twill weave. We have no difficulty in using the term texture for the cloth; it is just as applicable to type.

This analogy between typography and weaving will bear further study since there are a number of parallels which can be drawn between the appearances of the finished products of both arts.

In the weaving of textiles, the texture of the finished cloth is affected by any differences in the thickness of the threads used in the warp and in the weft, and by any variation in the space that separates these threads, in one direction or the other. The resulting differences in texture will be obvious – it does not take an expert in textiles to see the difference between a piece of silk and a coarse tweed.

The preceding paragraph could be rewritten, substituting the word 'lines' for threads and 'composition' for cloth, and we would have something like this: In the setting of type, the texture of the finished composition is affected by any differ ı ences in the thickness of the lines used in the vertical and the horizontal, and by any variation in the space that separates these lines, in one direction or the other. The resulting differ ı ences in texture will be obvious – it does not take an expert in typography to see the difference between a composition of Caslon and one of Futura Extrabold.

Basically this comparison means that if we use types which

PRINTING IS THE ART PRESERVATI

PRINTING IS THE ART PRESERVATIVE

printing is the art preservative of all the arts

PRINTING IS THE ART PRESERVAT

have very little contrast, or none, between their vertical and horizontal strokes, we will get a texture which can be compared to that of a plain weave; if we use a type which has a vertical emphasis, the texture of our typography will bear a resemblance of that of a corded fabric. A novelty type face like Barnum, which has its dominant stroke on the horizontal of the letter, will create a texture which seems to carry a heavy horizontal thread. The relative coarseness of our typographic threads will thus affect the texture of our line in exactly the same way as in textiles; we can get a 'silky' line with Caslon Old Style and a 'tweedy' line with a Clarendon Bold.

Just as silk and tweed have different physical weight in the hand, so a typographic line will also have different visual weights – a light weight with Caslon and a heavy one with Clarendon Bold. But the weight of the line is something which depends rather on the heaviness of the strokes of the individual letters and is independent of the textural relations. The Bodoni face has a vertical emphasis; we can retain this texture and increase the weight by using the Bodoni Bold or even Ultra Bodoni. Similarly, we can retain the textural quality we get in the plain weaves of the monotone strokes of Futura, and yet have different weights.

The typographic line, then, has two basic attributes in design; texture and weight. But it has one more characteristic that is important: its shape gives it a directional value. The typographic line is always roughly a rectangle, long and narrow; the sharpness of the rectangle it creates depends on whether the letters are uniform in height and alignment, as in the case of a line of capitals, or whether there are descenders and ascenders breaking the edges of the visual unit.

In either case, there is a directional movement, a flow along the line; this direction, because of the nature of typographic materials and our reading habits derived from Greco-Roman origins, is usually from left to right in a horizontal direction. There are times, however, when the requirement of good design will suggest that the direction be changed and that the line depart at varying angles, up or down, from our conventional horizontal reading direction. This change should only be made in display lines, where it can be accomplished without sacrificing legibility, where the matter so to be set is of secondary importance or, most important of all, where such a departure from the normal reinforces the sense of the copy.

The piling of letters one on top of the other should seldom, if ever, be used to create a vertical design. The varying widths of the letters ordinarily defy all attempts to create a clean rectangular shape; but even if that obstacle is successfully overcome the destruction of the normal horizontal word-pattern requires that the reader spell out the word to identify it.

This, then, is the typographic line, an element which has texture, weight, and direction; what texture, what weight, and what direction, will be determined by the nature of the subject and the over-all design concept in which the line is to be placed.

The title of a publication printed in Leipzig forms a vertical structural element at the hands of designer WALTER SCHILLER.

TYPO GRAFIE

7

Ein Buch wird um so mustergültiger, je reiner die einfache Schönheit der Typen in ihm zur Wirkung kommt. Aus ihr spricht, in ihr beruht, mit einem Worte, der Ruhm der Buchkunst. Und das mit Recht, denn einzig die Typen bestehen notwendig ganz durch sich selbst, alles übrige aber erst durch sie. Möchte doch diese Kunst, sinnvoll, nützlich und schön wie sie ist, auch allenthalben mit der ihrer würdigen Geschicklichkeit und Liebe geübt, mit Geschmack und gutem Urteil gefördert werden.   *Giambattista Bodoni*

Upper left, an unusual signature for the Massachusetts Institute of Technology suggests structural forms, where legibility is secondary to the pictorial value of the arrangement. Designed by WALTER PLATA. *At lower left, the sense of moving into, through, and out of a space is achieved by* BOB GILL. *The students of L'Ecole Estienne in Paris used the Brasilia type designed by* ALBERT HOLLENSTEIN *to create the textured typographical surface above.*

CASSIUS:

That you have wrong'd me doth appear in this:
You have condemn'd and noted Lucius Pella
For taking bribes here of the Sardians;
Wherein my letters, praying on his side,
Because I knew the man, were slighted off.
BRUTUS: You wrong'd yourself to write in such a case.
CASSIUS: In such a time as this it is not meet
That every nice offence should bear his comment.
BRUTUS: Let me tell you, Cassius, you yourself
Are much condemn'd to have an itching palm,
To sell and mart your offices for gold
To undeservers.
CASSIUS: I an itching palm?
You know that you are Brutus that speaks this,
Or, by the gods, this speech were else your last!
BRUTUS: The name of Cassius honours this corruption,
And chastisement doth therefore hide his head.
CASSIUS: Chastisement?
BRUTUS: Remember March; the ides of March remember.
Did not great Julius bleed for justice sake?
What villain touch'd his body that did stab
And not for justice? What, shall one of us,
That struck the foremost man of all this world
But for supporting robbers—shall we now
Contaminate our fingers with base bribes,
And sell the mighty space of our large honours
For so much trash as may be grasped thus?
I had rather be a dog and bay the moon
Than such a Roman.
CASSIUS: Brutus, bait not me!
I'll not endure it. You forget yourself

Quarrel
between
Brutus
and
Cassius

25

Julius
Caesar
Act 4
Scene III

[To hedge

the whole cloth

The line is to the mass what the threads are to the whole cloth. Like the weaver, the typographer has the option of knitting his lines together tightly, or loosening them up by 'leading' to let the horizontal movement of his lines create a different textural effect. The texture of a type face derives from the distribution of weight in each individual letter and the design of the letter itself. In the mass, each type face has its own textural and tactile individuality, as recognizable as the weave and feel of different types of cloth.

The decision whether or not to use leading will thus be determined to some extent by the textural qualities of the type itself; a 'plain weave' type like Caslon achieves its best effect when closely set in order to make the whole mass a tightly woven unit; a type like Bodoni with its vertical emphasis needs an open horizontal weave to improve legibility. Other factors, such as the length of the line, the amount of white let into the line by the length of the ascenders or descenders, and the weight of the face, may also dictate leading, and it is up to the designer to make a virtue of necessity by utilizing the textural effect as an integral part of the whole design concept.

In the mass, as in the line, the spacing between the words assumes great importance. The visual effect of lines of type set solid with wide spacing between the words, as compared with close word-spacing and leading between the lines, is demonstrated in the settings on the next page. The wide gaps in the first specimen tend to group the word units in a vertical direction; in the second specimen, the horizontal flow necessary for smooth reading is increased by closer spacing of the words and

Opposite page: a handsome typographic page woven into a rich, readable texture by MEYER WAGMAN *for one of the notable limited editions produced by Kurt H. Volk, New York.*

set solid It may be said of all printers that their job is to reproduce on paper the exact face of the letters which they have set into pages. This face is of a definite, constant and measurable size and shape; with any one press and any one paper there is a right and exact quan-

leaded 1 pt. It may be said of all printers that their job is to reproduce on paper the exact face of the letters which they have set into pages. This face is of a definite, constant and measurable size and shape; with any one press and any one paper there is a right and exact quantity of ink and pressure necessary to re-

leaded 2 pts. It may be said of all printers that their job is to reproduce on paper the exact face of the letters which they have set into pages. This face is of a definite, constant and measurable size and shape; with any one press and any one paper there is a right and exact quantity of ink and pressure necessary to re-

the underscoring channel of white space between the lines created by inserting leads. The type is the same in the two settings – only the distribution of space has been changed.

By this change in distribution of space the whole textural pattern is changed. Where the space between words exceeds the space between the lines, as it does in the first setting, the mass has a spotty, uneven texture; it is unpleasant to look at, and tiresome to read. The second setting has an even texture with a horizontal emphasis; it is designed for easy, comfortable reading. And like all things designed to be functional, it has its own aesthetic quality.

The accompanying double-page spread of specimen settings will demonstrate the individual qualities which each type design has in the mass. The text is deliberately gibberish so that the reader's attention will be directed not to the verbal content but to the appearance of the block of type. Each type face is shown two ways: set solid, and with a 2-point lead between the lines, so that a comparison may be made of the change in texture created by leading – for good or ill. To facilitate study of these blocks of type, it is recommended that the reader take a sheet of paper and cut out of the centre a rectangle a little larger than the type areas; each type block can then be seen through this opening isolated from adjoining specimens.

At this point, the relation of printing types to paper surfaces and printing methods must be briefly touched upon, for both influence the evaluation of texture in a type mass.

There are two basic printing processes which affect the ap pearance of type differently owing to their different natures:

1 *Letterpress printing* involves printing from a relief surface, such as printing type, and *impressing* the inked surface into the surface of the paper. Depending on the depth of that impres sion, the ink on the surface of the type will be squeezed to and beyond the edge of the actual letter, with the result that the inked impression will be bolder than the metal that made it.

2 *Offset lithographic printing* starts as a photographic process in which either a very light impression is produced by inked metal type and then photographed, or actual film images of letters are produced by photo-typesetting machines. The images are 'burned' into a metal plate which, when inked, transfers them to a rubber blanket by which they are in turn *laid on* the sheet of paper, rather than impressed into it.

There is a very wide range of paper surfaces, but for the pur poses of this discussion we shall restrict ourselves to three major categories:

1 *Antique papers* are papers with a soft, fibrous surface of which blotting paper is an extreme example. These are the papers most commonly used for book work and almost en tirely used in letterpress printing.

2 *Sized papers* are papers whose porous surfaces have been filled with a size to render them tougher, resistant to erasure, etc. They are used primarily for stationery. The sizing tends to resist ink pressed into the surface by letterpress, and it is very

The upper letter is an enlargement from a seventeenth-century Dutch book; below, the letter, again enlarged, from a modern letterpress impression on coated paper.

Hmne pobnioe nimhovinp ehot obapoha bemnlipa a entporhia anmnovih phoamehlmiv abonen ihnopobr pob hmnepob nioemin hovi penotoba pohab emnli r orhia amnovih pho amehlmiva bo nenihnopob reyuf minhovi pnontob apoh aoemnlipan imhoip obhmnft

VENETIAN: 10-pt. Bembo with 4-to-em word spacing

Hmne pobnioe nimhovinp ehot obapoha bel entporhia anmnovih phoamehlmiv abonenp pob hmnepob nioemin hovi penotoba pohab orhia amnovih pho amehlmiva bo nenihnop minhovi ponotob apoh aoemnlipan imhoip

VENETIAN: 10-pt. Palatino with 3-to-em word spacing

Hmne pobnioe nimhovinp ehot obapoha beu entporhia anmnovih phoamehlmiv abonen irt pob hmnepob nioemin hovi penotoba pohasf orhia amnovih pho amehlmiva bo nenihnopir minhovi ponotob apoh aoemnlipan imhoip rt

OLD STYLE: 10-pt. Garamond with 4-to-em word spacing

Hmne pobnioe nimhovinp ehot obapoha bejf entporhia anmnovih phoamehlmiv abonen ie pob hmnepob nioemin hovi penotoba pohabf orhia amnovih pho amehlmiva bo nenihnopo minhovi ponotob apoh aoemnlipan imhoip jr

OLD STYLE: 10-pt. Caslon with 4-to-em word spacing

Hmne pobnioe nimhovinp ehot obapoha bif entporhia anmnovih phoamehlmiv aboneno pob hmnepob nioemin hovi penotoba pohar orhia amnovih pho amehlmiva bo nenihnopi minhovi ponotob apoh aoemnlipan imhoipa

TRANSITIONAL: 10-pt. Scotch 4-to-em word spacing

Hmne pobnioe nimhovinp ehot obapoha bea entporhia anmnovih phoamehlmiv abonen ir pob hmnepob nioemin hovi penotoba pohaw orhia amnovih pho amehlmiva bo nenihnopt minhovi ponotob apoh aoemnlipan imhoip h

TRANSITIONAL: 10-pt. Baskerville 3-to-em word spacing

Hmne pobnioe nimhovinp ehot obapoha bei entporhia anmnovih phoamehlmiv abonenih pob hmnepob nioemin hovi penotoba pohab orhia amnovih pho amehlmiva bo nenihnopi minhovi ponotob apoh aoemnlipan imhoipoi

TRANSITIONAL: 10-pt. Caledonia 3-to-em word spacing

Hmne pobnioe nimhovinp ehot obapoha bemtf entporhia anmnovih phoamehlmiv abonen ihit pob hmnepob nioemin hovi penotoba pohab er orhia amnovih pho amehlmiva bo nenihnopoft minhovi ponotob apoh aoemnlipan imhoip obe

MODERN: 10-pt. Bodoni Book with 4-to-em word spacing

Hmne pobnioe nimhovinp ehot obapoha e entporhia anmnovih phoamehlmiv abonenc pob hmnepob nioemin hovi penotoba pofr orhia amnovih pho amehlmiva bo nenihnj minhovi ponotob apoh aoemnlipan imhois

MODERN: 10-pt. Century Expanded 3-to-em word spacing

Hmne pobnioe nimhovinp ehot s entporhia anmovih phoamehlme pob hmnepob nioemin hovi penc orhia amnovih pho amehlmiva n minhovi ponotob apoh aoemnliif

EGYPTIAN: 10-pt. Craw Clarendon 3-to-em word spacing

Hmne pobnioe nimhovinp ehot obapoha brt entporhia anmnovih phoamehlmiv abonen il pob hmnepob nioemin hovi penotoba pohai orhia amnovih pho amehlmiva bo nenihnots minhovi pnontob apoh aoemnlipa imhoiprto

SANS SERIF: 10-pt. Univers 55 with 3-to-em word spacing

Hmne pobnioe nimhovinp ehot obapoe entporhia anmnovih phoamehlmiv abiz pob hmnepob nioemin hovi penotoba f orhia amnovih pho amehlmiva bo neng minhovi ponotob apoh aoemnlipan imr

SANS SERIF: 10-pt. Univers 75 with 3-to-em word spacing

Hmne pobnioe nimhovinp ehot obapoha bemnlipa a
entporhia anmnovih phoamehlmiv abonen ihnopobr
pob hmnepob nioemin hovi penotoba pohab emnli r
orhia amnovih pho amehlmiva bo nenihnopob reyuf

VENETIAN: 10-pt. Bembo with 4-to-em word spacing

Hmne pobnioe nimhovinp ehot obapoha bel
entporhia anmnovih phoamehlmiv abonenp
pob hmnepob nioemin hovi penotoba pohab
orhia amnovih pho amehlmiva bo nenihnop

VENETIAN: 10-pt. Palatino with 3-to-em word spacing

Hmne pobnioe nimhovinp ehot obapoha beu
entporhia anmnovih phoamehlmiv abonen irt
pob hmnepob nioemin hovi penotoba pohasf
orhia amnovih pho amehlmiva bo nenihnopir

OLD STYLE: 10-pt. Garamond with 4-to-em word spacing

Hmne pobnioe nimhovinp ehot obapoha bejf
entporhia anmnovih phoamehlmiv abonen ie
pob hmnepob nioemin hovi penotoba pohabf
orhia amnovih pho amehlmiva bo nenihnopo

OLD STYLE: 10-pt. Caslon with 4-to-em word spacing

Hmne pobnioe nimhovinp ehot obapoha bif
entporhia anmnovih phoamehlmiv aboneno
pob hmnepob nioemin hovi penotoba pohar
orhia amnovih pho amehlmiva bo nenihnop

TRANSITIONAL: 10-pt. Scotch 4-to-em word spacing

Hmne pobnioe nimhovinp ehot obapoha bea
entporhia anmnovih phoamehlmiv abonen ir
pob hmnepob nioemin hovi penotoba pohaw
orhia amnovih pho amehlmiva bo nenihnopt

TRANSITIONAL: 10-pt. Baskerville 3-to-em word spacing

Hmne pobnioe nimhovinp ehot obapoha bei
entporhia anmnovih phoamehlmiv abonenih
pob hmnepob nioemin hovi penotoba pohab
orhia amnovih pho amehlmiva bo nenihnopi

TRANSITIONAL: 10-pt. Caledonia 3-to-em word spacing

Hmne pobnioe nimhovinp ehot obapoha bemtf
entporhia anmnovih phoamehlmiv abonen ihit
pob hmnepob nioemin hovi penotoba pohab er
orhia amnovih pho amehlmiva bo nenihnopoft

MODERN: 10-pt. Bodoni Book with 4-to-em word spacing

Hmne pobnioe nimhovinp ehot obapoha e
entporhia anmovih phoamehlmiv abonenc
pob hmnepob nioemin hovi penotoba pofr
orhia amnovih pho amehlmiva bo nenihnj

MODERN: 10-pt. Century Expanded 3-to-em word spacing

**Hmne pobnioe nimhovinp ehot s
entporhia anmovih phoamehlme
pob hmnepob nioemin hovi penc
orhia amnovih pho amehlmiva n**

EGYPTIAN: 10-pt. Craw Clarendon 3-to-em word spacing

Hmne pobnioe nimhovinp ehot obapoha brt
entporhia anmnovih phoamehlmiv abonen il
pob hmnepob nioemin hovi penotoba pohai
orhia amnovih pho amehlmiva bo nenihnots

SANS SERIF: 10-pt. Univers 55 with 3-to-em word spacing

**Hmne pobnioe nimhovinp ehot obapoe
entporhia anmnovih phoamehlmiv abiz
pob hmnepob nioemin hovi penotoba f
orhia amnovih pho amehlmiva bo neng**

SANS SERIF: 10-pt. Univers 75 with 3-to-em word spacing

difficult to get crisp, clean impressions by other than the offset lithographic process.

3 *Calendared, filled, and coated papers*: The terms cover a very wide range of those papers in most common commercial use in printing and magazine publishing today. The surfaces of these papers are all smoothed by being passed over heated metal cylinders at the end of the paper-making process; some of them have fillers added to the pulp, such as titanium to increase whiteness, or kaolin (china clay) to give coated papers their lustre. These papers require less impression by letterpress than the previously mentioned papers; many of them are particu larly adapted to offset lithographic printing.

It should be obvious from this discussion, however inade quate it may be to treat so complex a subject, that a type printed by letterpress *into* a bulky antique paper will look quite different *laid on* a highly finished sheet by offset.

As a consequence, it would be a mistake to admire a page of Caslon printed by letterpress into a soft, absorbent antique paper, and expect to get the same rich result in another job run by offset on a highly glazed sheet of paper. Conversely, the crisp appearance of a modern sans serif letter printed by offset on a coated sheet in a type specimen book will not indicate the sorry irregularity its contours will have if printed by letterpress on an antique or sized paper.

Experience will teach the designer what process and what papers are best suited to each type face; until the experience is gained, he would do well to ask his paper supplier to show him specimens of his favourite types on a variety of papers, and then make his judgments from these samples.

However, some idea of the textures of different types can be got from the spread previously referred to if it is borne in mind that the types were printed by offset on a dull coated paper from reproduction proofs printed from type. If the spreads had been printed by letterpress, all types would have been a little heavier, and the crispness of detail would have been a little less sharp (depending on the amount of the impression); if they had been printed by letterpress on an antique paper, they would have been considerably deeper in overall tonal value, and their outlines would have been far less sharp.

Having studied the textural characteristics of the type mass, we must now consider the use of mass as an element in design. Mass is not only an area of words; it may consist of a single large dominating letter, a group of display lines, a trade-mark, an area of colour, or even a plain type rule.

The dominant characteristic of any mass is, of course, its shape, the area it defines against the white of the paper. Because typography is for the greater part limited to horizontal and vertical elements, mass will generally appear as a rectangle or a square. The exception to this is the individual letter which has its own contour, and the trade mark which has a shape con ferred on it by a designer.

By and large, the very limitation to the horizontal and ver tical is typography's greatest asset; it compels the designer in type to maintain a Spartan simplicity of pattern and to avoid the tendency to over-elaboration which plagues those designers working in less rigid mediums. Simple geometric masses are the forms most natural to typography; they should be accepted at face value and used to advantage.

Even the early scribes accepted the rigid framework of the page – their work area was squared off on the page before the quill touched the parchment – and their meticulous script was kept within its geometric boundaries. Any urge to elaboration was confined to initials and to marginal decoration which em phasized and provided contrast to the rectangular character of the written areas. Gutenberg's first Bible established a beautiful repetition of the vertical shape of the Gothic letter, and the vertical structure of each of the two columns of type gave two upright masses in a rectangular area.

L'image

n'est pas toujours
ce que l'on voit
mais
ce que l'on ressent.

Two vertical axes, one at the far left, and one internally, give this setting a free form that helps emphasize the message. Designed by RENÉ TOUTAIN, *Paris.*

But there are times when the cause of good design is better served if a mass assumes a free form instead of geometric rigid ity. Sometimes the meaning of the words of a display heading is given greater emphasis if the mass is asymmetrical and irregular in outline. As always, the nature and meaning of the copy should take precedence over dogmatic design require ments. A personal whim of the designer no less than the rigid page can be a Procrustean bed, torturing type by violating its inherent qualities. A free-shaped area, wherever it occurs, must be a spontaneous and natural typographic expression of the copy; the copy should almost insist, of its own accord, that it be set in this way. There are few more revolting sights than lines of type that have been alternately jammed tight and spaced out in order to square up a block of copy, or type that is painfully contoured to form a picture silhouette. Usually effects so grimly worked out are not worth the time and skill spent on them.

The type rules and type ornaments which are part of the stock in trade of every printing shop offer endless opportuni ties for experimentation in the creation of mass areas with new and exciting textures. It requires no great creative imagination to see the possibilities inherent in the use of type rule as back ground material. By using printed rules of varying widths and thus changing the widths of the emergent white stripes, spatial relationships may be altered. Typographic squares, spots, tri angles, stars, diamonds, even letters and words, have the same potential ability to become either over-all background patterns or masses of required shapes occupying defined areas.

The 'mass' in typography is a homogeneous unit which is organized as an expression of subject-matter, as a component part of it, or as a background to it. It has qualities of texture, weight, and form, all of which undergo variations and are comprised of few or many units welded into an indivisible unity.

Opposite: the French painter VICTOR VASARELY *explores the texture and spatial relationships of simple lines in a manner that should stimulate printers and designers ('Teke', 1956).*

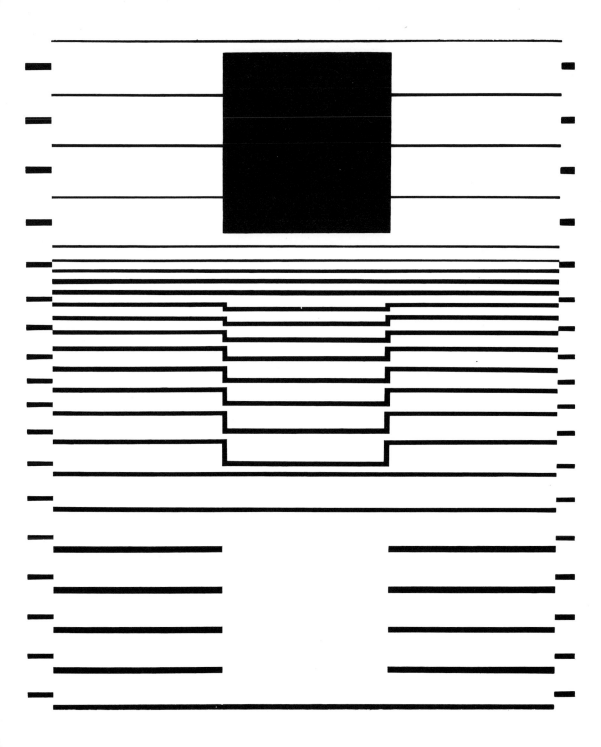

fipunculo per ilquale emanaua laqua della fontana per artificio perpe
tua in la fubiecta concha.

Nel Patore dunque di quefto uafo promineua uno pretiofiffimo mõ
ticulo, mirabilmente congefto di innumere gemme globofe preffamente
una ad laltra coaceruate, cum inæquale, o uero rude deformatura, lepidif
fimamente il mõticulo fcrupeo rendeuano, cũ corrufcatiõe di uarii fulge
tri di colore, cum proportionata eminẽtia . Nel uertice, o uero cacumine
di quefto monticulo, nafceua uno arbufculo di mali punici, di tronco, o
uero ftipite & di rami, & fimilmente tutto quefto compofito di oro prælu
cente. Le foglie appofitie di fcintillãte Smaragdo. Gli fructi alla granditu
dine naturale difperfamente collocati, cum il fidio doro ifchiantati larga
mente, & in loco degli grani ardeuano nitidiffimi rubini, fopra omni pa
ragonio nitidiffimi di craffitudine fabacea· Pofcia lo ingeniofo fabro di
quefta inextimabile factura & copiofo effendo del fuo difcorfo
imaginario hauea difcriminato, in loco di Cico gli grani cum
tenuiffima bractea argentea .   Oltra di quefto & ragioneuol
mente hauea ficto & alcuni altri mali crepati , ma di
granelatura immaturi, oue hauea cõpofito cum im
probo exquifito di craffi unione di candore orienta
le. Ancora folertemente hauea fincto gli balau
fti facti di perfecto coralio in calici pieni di api
ci doro. Vltra di quefto fora della fum
mitate del fiftulatamente uacuo ftipite
ufciua uno uerfatile & libero fty
lo, il cardine imo delqua
le, era fixo in uno ca
po peronato, o ue
ramente firma
to fopra il medio
dellaxide. & afcendeua
per il peruio & inftobato trunco.

DIVINE TO EAT, EASY TO MAKE, AND
BEAUTIFUL TO LOOK ON: ELEGANT PAR-
FAITS. THERE ARE TWO TYPES: THE
FRENCH, WHICH IS A CREAMY, DEL-
ICATE, COOL (BUT NOT ICY) MIX-
TURE WITH A BASE OF SUGAR,
EGGS, CREAM, FRUIT AND/OR
FLAVORINGS; AND THE AMERI-
CAN, MADE WITH COMMERCIAL
ICE CREAMS OR SHERBETS OR
BOTH WITH A SURPRISE INGRE-
DIENT, SUCH AS FRUITS, COR-
DIALS, COGNAC, NUTS, SAUCES
(SEE McCALL'S FINE SAUCE
RECIPES ON PAGE 00). WITH
AMERICAN PARFAITS, YOUR
IMAGINATION CAN HAVE FREE
REIN. WITH THE FRENCH, HOW-
EVER, YOU MUST FOLLOW REC-
IPE DIRECTIONS TO THE
LETTER. PARFAIT MEANS, OF
COURSE, PERFECT, AND WE
CAN IMAGINE FEW MORE PER-
FECT DESSERTS, ESPECIALLY
IF YOU WANT TO SHOW OFF.
FOR THESE ARE TRULY SHOW-
OFF RECIPES! FROM THE
COOK'S STANDPOINT, THERE
IS A REAL ADVANTAGE IN SERV-
ING FROZEN DESSERTS. FOR
THE OBVIOUS REASON, THEY
MUST BE MADE WELL AHEAD
AND REFRIGERATED. THUS,
THE BIG DESSERT PROBLEM
IS OUT OF THE WAY WHEN IT'S
TIME TO PREPARE THE MAIN
PART OF THE MEAL. AT FAR
RIGHT, YOU SEE AN AMER-
ICAN PARFAIT, VANILLA
ICE CREAM LAYERED
WITH PISTACHIO
AND TOPPED
WITH WAL-
NUTS AND
WHIPPED
C R E A M.
THE STRAW-
BERRY AND
A P R I C O T
P A R F A I T S
ARE BOTH
CLASSIC
F R E N C H.
FOR THE RECIPES,
TURN TO PAGE 00, WHERE
YOU WILL FIND THE FRENCH AS WELL
AS GOOD VARIATIONS OF THE QUICK
AND POPULAR AMERICAN PARFAITS.
THEN, PLAN A PARTY.

Two designers, five centuries apart: left, ALDUS MANUTIUS, *Venice 1499; right,* OTTO STORCH, McCall's Magazine.

Up to this point we have been discussing the 'elements' of typography: those forms, or aggregations of forms, which cohere in a visual unit. The basic element was the single character, and when it entered into definite relationships with other characters, a new element was created, the word. The words, in turn, combined into the line, and the line into the mass.

Each of these elements has so far been considered in isolation; they have been studied for all their intrinsic and individual qualities and characteristics. The time has now come to study them in relation to each other.

This is the point where contemporary typography has departed from the classical patterns which had characterized the best work of the first half millennium of the art of printing. Why and in what way has that departure been effected? Our predecessors knew and understood the refinements of letter forms and of the texture of a page of type, and they used their knowledge skilfully, to create handsome books. Why should we depart from the practice they established through centuries of fine printing?

The answer is not far to seek. It lies in the difference in the uses to which the printed word is put today. The concern of the old master printers was to print books, to make widely available the knowledge and the literature which, before the invention of printing, had been the monopoly of those few who could afford a hand-written book. Printing put books within the reach of many; and the task of setting to type and paper all the classics of literature, all the scientific knowledge of accumulated centuries, the works of Scripture and the legal

codes, was a staggering one in which many scholars and crafts ⌐
men were engaged for the first few hundred years of printing.
They designed fine books that stand today as models of the
typographic art.

Books are, of course, still an important part of today's print ⌐
ing industry, but they are part only, not the whole. The rise
of our contemporary industrial civilization has made new de ⌐
mands on printing, demands that are associated with the dis ⌐
tribution and marketing of the steady stream of commodities
that our highly efficient industries produce.* Printing that
must do this kind of job cannot look the same as the printing
which suits a book. A book does not have to demand to be
read – but an advertisement does. An advertisement is an impo ⌐
sition on a busy individual's time and attention, for which
there is today a tremendous amount of competition. Twentieth-
century man is besieged with beckoning attractions – moving
pictures, plays, radio, concerts, television, newspapers, maga ⌐
zines, books, the lure of the highway and distant places – and
into this carnival of attractions, printing enters to try to sell
him a thousand different commodities and services. Can this
task of printing be compared with the task of printing books
that faced the first printers? The quiet typography of books
designed to give a man comfortable reading in leisure hours in
his home is not adequate for selling wares in the visual hubbub
of the marketplace. The modern book publisher recognizes
this when he clothes his trade books in jackets designed to
compete for attention at the booksellers': such books must now
demand to be bought, at least.

It was the nineteenth-century printer who was first con ⌐

---

*This is not intended as an assessment of the comparative social con ⌐
tribution of the two forms. Knowing from first-hand experience the
meagre budgets available for the printing of low-cost school text ⌐
books in underdeveloped areas of the world, the author has come to
some conclusions unsympathetic to large advertising budgets.

SYMBOLA

HEROICA

M. CLAVDII PARADINI,

BELLIIOCENSIS

CANONICI,

ET D. GABRIELIS SYMEONIS.

*Multo, quàm antea, fidelius de Gallica lingua
in Latinam conuersa.*

ANTVERPIAE.

Ex officina Chriſtophori Plantini.

M. D. LXVII.

CVM PRIVILEGIO.

fronted with this demand on his skill. He turned to strong display and decoration as a means of attracting attention to the message. Highly decorative types and ornaments were cut to meet the demand for something new and different; printers competed among themselves to see how many different type faces could be jammed into the setting of a single message; type founders cut large wood type, hoping that sheer size would overpower the reader; compositors outdid themselves in bending and twisting their rules and type lines, only to produce a typographic wreckage.

Printers were not alone in this orgy of decoration. The intro duction of machines had brought about mass production which at first imitated the hand craftsmanship that preceded it. The skill of the artist in wood and metal and glass was crudely adapted to the limitations of the machine, and the results found a ready sale among the newly rich merchants and members of the industrial class. Lacking essential good taste, these people were building and furnishing their homes in imitation of an earlier grandeur—but with shoddy results. The ornamental work done by the wood-carver or the ironmonger or the hand weaver cannot be performed by a machine. With its charac teristic unvarying precision the machine finds its most eco nomical and artistic use in the production of commodities of structural simplicity and unornamented surface. It is only necessary to compare any machine-produced commodity to day with one of fifty years ago to realize that this truth, though slow in dawning, is finally being accepted.

Typography, too, has tidied itself up, but it has done so by returning to its more dignified classical forms. It has not pioneered new concepts that would fit the new methods of the machine. It remained for typography's sister arts to undertake the pioneering: painting, sculpture, and architecture left tradi tion to blaze new trails in visual presentation. From them printing has learned how to use its own materials, its own

elements, in the context of modern technology. Design has returned to rescue typography from Victorian ugliness and post-Victorian mediocrity.

Design, to define it very briefly, is the art of assembling diverse elements into an organized unit. The problem is just the same in typography as it is in the manufacture of industrial products. The watchmaker must assemble tiny cogs and gears and springs into a circular or rectangular case, the car manufacturer must assemble wheels, engine, transmission, steering apparatus, gears, fuel storage, into a sleek, upholstered living-room in motion. Typographic design, too, takes diverse elements and organizes them into a visual unit. And this brings us back to where we started this chapter: the beginning of a study of the relations between elements.

The objective of typographic design is to organize all of the elements of communication into a harmonious and unified whole, either by achieving a quiet uniformity of similar elements or by the visually exciting use of contrasting ones. What determines the result is the way in which the diverse elements are organized in relation to each other, the contributions each makes to form, texture, and weight, and the effect of their relation with the space in which they exist.

We must ask then: what kind of elements are put together, where, and in what way? These three questions are the basic ones in any discussion of relationships. For simplicity, they may be broken down in this way:

What kind of elements? relationships of concord and contrast.

Where? relationships in space.

In what way? relationships of structure.

The basic form of the relationship between typographic elements is determined when the designer decides whether there is to be uniformity of appearance and form or a contrast of one element with another. Between complete concord and complete, stark contrast there are, of course, many intermediate stages, and an ability to achieve concord in general effect while introducing subtle contrasts in specific effects gives a designer his greatest opportunity for typographic variety.

What do we mean by concord and contrast in the context of typography?

Concord is the result of the blending of typographic elements to give a uniform impression; colour, texture, size, proportions and affinity of the type faces combine to produce this effect. The traditional book form is the classic example of concord: it is found in both the uniform, tightly woven, dense pages of the Gutenberg Bible and the light, open, gray pages of the conventional contemporary book set in roman types.

To achieve complete concord, all the elements must have the same characteristics; a single family of type must be used throughout (though sizes may vary), and any borders and decorative material must match this type in tonal value. The relationships of the white areas must be carefully balanced; there must be proper proportion between the white spaces inside the block of type and those surrounding it, so that a harmony is achieved.

Concord does not necessarily imply a light tonal value. If the prevailing tone is struck by the use of a light roman face, then border or decorative material will certainly echo that

A type page which is completely harmonious in all its elements – border, decoration, and type, as well as the white space within it.

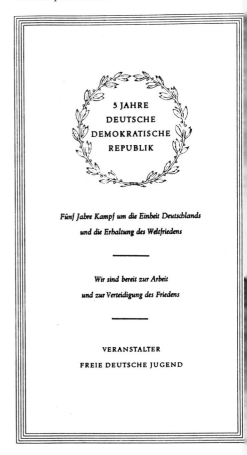

5 JAHRE
DEUTSCHE
DEMOKRATISCHE
REPUBLIK

*Fünf Jahre Kampf um die Einheit Deutschlands
und die Erhaltung des Weltfriedens*

*Wir sind bereit zur Arbeit
und zur Verteidigung des Friedens*

VERANSTALTER
FREIE DEUTSCHE JUGEND

DEUTSCHE KUNSTSCHAU

HALBMONATS-ZEITSCHRIFT FÜR DAS GESAMTE
KUNSTLEBEN DEUTSCHLANDS
MUSIK·THEATER·TANZ·LITERATUR·BILDENDE
KÜNSTE·VEREINSWESEN·MIT VIELEN BILDERN
HERAUSGEGEBEN VON
HANS WERNER GÖTTIG·FRANKFURT AM MAIN
VERLAG VON J. ANDRE·OFFENBACH AM MAIN
DER BEZUGSPREIS BETRÄGT MONATLICH 1 MK.

*Another setting in which complete harmony prevails,
but this time in greater density of colour, employing*
RUDOLF KOCH'S *hand-cut Neuland type.*

tonal value, and white areas will be generous. Similarly the even gray texture of such a face would be repeated in the uniform lines and density of colour in the illustrations. But concord can be achieved using black-face types, provided again that the density of the type is picked up in the other elements in the composition, and that the white areas are in turn balanced off against it. A type like Bodoni has within itself an interplay of thick and thin lines; a border of parallel thick and thin lines or an illustration with thick and thin pen strokes will be in concord with the type.

Contrast is the opposite of concord; it is based on a unity of differences.

We understand the surroundings in which we live through contrast; all of our senses react to contrast. We understand shadow because we know about light; differences in qualities are measured by contrast; soft and hard, sweet and sour, rough and smooth, cold and warm, light and heavy. Our senses are trained to detect the differences between things in the world about us. The act of reading itself is possible because of contrast: the contrast between the colour of the paper and the colour of the ink, and if the contrasts are weakened through paper and ink being too close in colour, or through the characteristics of individual letters not being clearly defined, legibility is reduced. We depend on contrast for easy reading.

Contrast to be effective must be sharp; timidity in employing contrast will defeat its whole purpose and will result only in conflict. It is a popular belief that matrimonial success depends on a complete contrast of personalities; that people of too similar temperaments will be involved sooner or later in a conflict of personalities. It can be left to the marriage counsellors to determine the truth of the adage, but it is most certainly applicable in typography.

Two old-style roman types with only slight dissimilarities will be in conflict; they are not similar enough to establish

typography is an ART

TYPOGRAPHY IS AN **ART**

TYPOGRAPHY IS AN *art*

At the top, Caslon roman capitals and lower case italic of the same face establish harmonious relationships. The line in the centre is in a state of conflict between the old style Garamond caps and the modern Bodoni display. At the bottom the structures of the sans serif caps and the large old style italics are sufficiently differentiated to create a pleasant contrast.

concord, nor different enough to set up contrast. There can be no compromise between *almost* similar elements, but it is possible to interweave concord and contrast. It is possible, for example, to make use in a design of two letters of the same type face but of substantially different sizes: they are in contrast as to size, but their structures are in concord; the result is harmony.

Similarly, a roman type and a script type may have in common a structure based on thick and thin strokes – Bodoni and Bank Script provide an example. Their basic structures are in concord, but the vertical roman type and the strongly sloped and rounded forms of the script produce a contrast of form; the two faces are in complete harmony. One may carry this latter example a stage further. If the italic form of Bodoni were to be used with Bank Script type, the essential harmony would be destroyed; the two sloped letters would be in conflict with each other, and neither concord nor contrast of form would be achieved, even though the concord of structure (thick and thin lines) was maintained.

It will be useful at this point to establish all of the dimensions in which concord or contrast can be used with typographical material, and then discuss each of these dimensions individually in their practical application to the daily problems of the design of commercial printing. These dimensions are:

a / the dimension of size

b / the dimension of weight

c / the dimension of letter structure

d / the dimension of form

e / the dimension of colour

f / the dimension of texture

g / the dimension of direction.

Like the seven notes of the musical scale, these seven dimensions of concord or contrast can form the basis of the most varied compositions.

The first five dimensions listed are those in which the basic letters can be contrasted to one another; the other two require larger units of words, lines, or masses. If we take just the first four, and study the chart which has been prepared of all the potential combinations of concord and contrast in these four dimensions (fourteen in all), we will see what an important principle of typographic design is embodied in the theory of concord and contrast and what new horizons of design are opened up to anyone who masters it.

The interplay of concord and contrast in the hands of imaginative designers is currently producing some of the most stimulating and visually appealing typography in the history of printing. The student or enthusiast who takes the trouble to analyse the works shown in current catalogues and typographic exhibitions can learn what concords and contrasts the designers employed to achieve their effects.

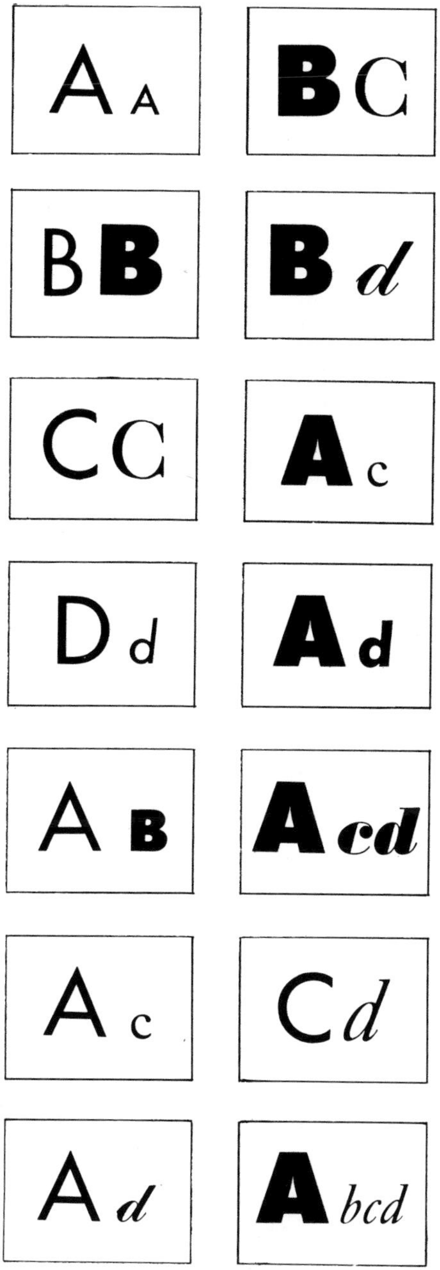

Contrast of size

A A

Contrast of weight and structure

B C

Contrast of weight

B **B**

Contrast of weight, structure, and form

B *d*

Contrast of structure

C C

Contrast of size, weight, and structure

A c

Contrast of form

D d

Contrast of size and form

A **d**

Contrast of size and weight

A **B**

Contrast of size, structure, and form

A *cd*

Contrast of size and structure

A c

Contrast of structure and form

C *d*

Contrast of size, structure, and form

A *d*

Contrast of size, weight, structure, and form

A *bcd*

The very fact that we have the typographic terms 'display size' and 'body size' indicates the integral role in design of contrast of size. Gutenberg cut the first type in a single size, but he employed scribes to set in large initials with his body type: he thus achieved contrast of size. The technique has been employed ever since, right down to the modern tabloid newspaper whose front page lets out a 144-pt. scream to tell the public about the event which has unnerved the editor that day.

As with contrasts in all dimensions, contrast in size is only effective when used with discretion. Not that the differences in size should be slight – far from it; the caution simply means that effects dependent on size cannot be achieved if there is too much large type; the smaller, and contrasting, element will be unable to break through and contribute its share.

A safe rule of thumb to follow is to make the areas occupied by the contrasting elements approximately equal: for example, a single large letter might be followed by a word or words which have about the same general weight as a unit of the large type, or a large word might be followed by a line which has the same weight. The initial should never exceed the inking area of the contrasting form unless it is cut down in weight through the use of colour. A single letter of 72-pt. Futura Ultrabold, for example, would lose weight without losing size if run in a pale tint, while the smaller unit was run in black.

The cost of fonts of large types often prevents a medium-size or small printing plant from having an adequate selection of large letters for display as initials. However, digging around among old fonts of wood type which are gathering dust in

Opposite page: a typographical exercise by GERHARD SCHNEIDER, *a student at the Werkkunstschule, Offenbach am Main.*

The device used by the Institute of Contemporary Art, London, defines only the outer and inner shapes of the letters with simple rules. Below, an advertisement by THEO DIMSON, *Toronto, exploits strong contrast of size and texture, and vigorous opposition of vertical and horizontal.*

seldom-used cases of some shops will often unearth striking old letters which are decorative and effective if run in colour. Moreover, large display letters can often be made up from type material with the expenditure of a bit of imagination and a little labour. Type rules and squares are most convenient to use, and they can be worked up into solid letters, shaded letters, shaded letters with shadow edges, or open letters defined only by rules cut to indicate a shadow. Reverse letters can be built up in the same way, by setting the rules or squares in a rectangular shape and cutting away from the rules the shape of the letter, by removing the squares to leave the reverse letter, or by using type material to define only the outer and inner shapes of the letters. The background grid effect created by the

"Something moves as it has never moved before in this land, moves dumbly in the deepest runnels of a collective mind, yet by sure direction toward a known goal. Sometimes by thought, more often by intuition, the Canadian people make the final discovery. They are discovering themselves. That passion of discovery which once sent birchbark canoes down unmapped waters, pushed railways across the Rockies, and dragged men to the frozen seas turns inward to explore a darker terrain. The nation labors in the travail of self-discovery and, by this labor, proves that it is in truth a nation, the home of a people." This advertisement, commemorating the completion of the St. Lawrence Seaway and Power Project, and its official opening by Her Majesty, Elizabeth II, is published by **THE TORONTO-DOMINION BANK**

From "Canada: Tomorrow's Giant" by Bruce Hutchison   Published by Longmans, Green and Company

failure of the type squares to meet can be effective in itself. Of course there are always the services of the photo-engraver who can be called upon to enlarge a proof of a smaller face, or to supply a zinc of a hand-drawn letter.

The applications of contrast in size are almost universal; there is scarcely a job where a large letter or word cannot be used to striking effect. To take business stationery, the initial letter of the main name or product name, if set large and run in a second colour, can provide a focal point around which it is easy to organize the subordinate material; this pattern can be used on all sorts of forms, from the letterhead and envelope to the business card. Monograms of two or more initials can accomplish the same purpose and may well serve to establish a striking trade mark.

Cover designs of all kinds lend themselves to this treatment of mass: menus, with the word 'menu' set large as a back-ground to the name of the restaurant using it; catalogues, with either the word 'catalogue' or the name or initial of the firm dominating the cover; price lists, with a similar treatment; house organs, with the name of the publication made large enough to form a solid panel of its own; announcements, with the initial 'A' establishing a starting point for the message.

Very often the repetition of an initial letter at different angles can create a pattern which is interesting either in itself or as a symbol of the business indicated. But each problem calls for the application of ingenuity, and it is only possible here to give fictitious examples. Effective application of the principle of contrast of size can only be made if the designer studies his copy for the clue that will indicate what letter or word can take this distortion and still be effective both as a design and, if possible, as a symbol. Sometimes a little doodling on a scrap of paper will help an idea come to life. At this stage the type indication does not have to be meticulous, so long as a contrast is there to start images of all sorts of possibilities flashing across the mind.

Typographic "doodles" achieved by photo-typsetting at the studio of ALBERT HOLLENSTEIN *in Paris.*

TONNAGE

When is a heavy weight of advertising dollars bound to succeed? And when is "Tonnage" bound to fail? Is the smartest advertiser the one with the biggest budget? If you look at the history of advertising, you will observe the following facts: There are advertisers who slackened, or weakened their efforts (sometimes at critical times) and the results can be seen in the forgotten trademarks of the past. On the other hand, there are advertisers who mounted massive advertising campaigns—costing many millions of dollars—who have failed to increase their sales. The question of the advertising appropriation should always be preceded by these questions: Do I have an idea which will sell my product? Has my agency been thorough enough to arrive at a sound selling strategy, and ingenious enough to express it in an arresting and interesting way? If the answers to these questions are "yes," advertising tonnage can be regarded as an investment, instead of an expense. Everything depends on the idea. Ideas sell products because—people buy ideas.

New York • Chicago • Detroit • San Francisco • Los Angeles • Hollywood • Montreal • Toronto • London • Mexico City • Frankfurt • San Juan • Caracas • Geneva **YOUNG & RUBICAM • ADVERTISING**

When we speak of the weight of a letter, we are speaking, of course, of the thickness of the lines that compose it; or, to put it another way,. of the relation between the printed area and the white of the paper. If the printed area is much less than that of paper which shows through and around it, the letter is considered light; on the other hand, if the area of ink which it deposits almost fills the total area it occupies, as a Futura Ultra bold letter does, it is considered heavy. Light and heavy are contrasts as effective as night and day, as highlight and shadow.

The creation of light and dark areas within a drawing is an effective device used by artists to dramatize their subject, and it is called chiaroscuro (from Italian, *chiaro*, light, and *scuro*, dark). In typography the device can be just as effective even if it has not been honoured by such a fine-sounding word.

Just as in the use of contrast of size, there is no real middle ground in the use of contrast of weight; it is black face against light face, or it is ineffective. Fortunately, as in the human family, many members of our type families have their black brothers – Bodoni has its Ultra Bodoni, the sans serifs their extrabold versions, Egyptians have their heavy weight. Besides these members of regular type families, many other black-face types have been designed which will harmonize in structure with standard faces. A word of caution is in order here: the regular run of bold faces which have been cut as companions to some of the old classic faces do not effectively contrast with them; at best they provide a slight emphasis, but more often than not they look as if they had illegitimately sprung from the classic parent face: they appear to be merely battered-down types used too long and ready for the hellbox.

Opposite page: a dramatic example of contrast of weight – with the added impact of direction contrast (see page 74). Designed by DONALD EGENSTEINER *of New York.*

Contrast of weight, by itself, has many applications, whose chief purpose is to give emphasis. Within a display line, a single word can be given prominence and importance by a change to black-face letters. An initial letter of a firm name or a product name can provide a hub for a signature if it is set in a black version while the rest of the name is in light face, or vice versa.

When you can have more, why take less?

JOHN AVERILL, *the late Chicago cartoonist, typographer, and proprietor of the Molehill Press whose publication,* Seed Corn, *won international fame, was a master of the use of contrast of weight, as indicated by this advertisement done over a quarter of a century ago.*

Contrasts of weight can also be brought into play between two different materials. No one has employed this technique more effectively than the artist-typographer John Averill, of Chicago, who used Caslon Old Style accented by a solid black rule in combination with his own inimitable drawings, which are dominantly black, in a series of advertisements.

The relation between a heavy line of black-face type and the ample white space in which it is set can likewise produce a contrast of weight. The effect suggests a comparison with that produced by a dirty thumb-print against a newly plastered wall – against a background of pristine whiteness the offending print attracts the eye out of all proportion to its size or impor tance. Similarly, contrasts between headings and text matter and the white areas of paper can create three distinct weights: the black bar of the heading poised against the light gray mass of the text, and the two set in a generous area of white. Some of the simplest and most striking typographical designs have been based on no more than this relationship.

One of the most familiar uses of contrast by means of black-face type is for subheadings in continuous text. The contrast provides direction signs for the reader looking for specific information. Such headings can be handled in two ways: set in an open break between paragraphs or run into the paragraph at the beginning, with the text continuing from the end of the heading. The latter is a useful device where space does not permit sacrificing the area which could be occupied by several lines of type just to let in a heading. If these black-face run-ins are extended slightly into the left-hand margin, they are even more easily picked up by the skimming eye. Or they can be set entirely in the margin, flush right to, and aligning at the top with, the paragraphs to which they refer.

DIRECTIONS: pour the fluid directly on the garment or textile to be cleaned; rub gently with a circular motion while it is slowly penetrating the fabric

taken every step to insure that the tourist will have every convenience.

HIGHWAY ROUTE: Take Number 10 highway to Corners, then turn left along Number 33 until

On business stationery and business cards, black-face can be used to bring out an important word or words. Quick identi fication of the nature of a business form can often be helped when a boldface label in an upper corner proclaims an 'invoice' or a 'purchase order'.

An index is often made easier to use if each new alphabetical grouping starts with a black-face letter, either set on a separate line or simply set as the first letter of the first word of each alphabetic group.

In catalogues, annual reports, price lists, programmes, direc tories – indeed in any printing job you care to name – weight has an important part to play if used with discretion.

Tg

Here again a definition is in order, so that there may be no confusion between 'structure' and 'form,' which is taken up in the next section. To clarify the difference between them, take the example of a capital T and a lower case g, both of the Futura family. Their forms are entirely different; one consists of straight lines at right angles and the other of rounded forms: the forms are in contrast. But each of them is composed of lines of the same weight throughout; structurally they are in concord.

Basically, all types fall into either one or the other of two structural groups: (*a*) the group which includes the sans serif and square serif and also certain monotone scripts whose main distinguishing feature is that there is no variation, or a very slight variation, in the weight of the strokes which comprise the letter; and (*b*) the group which includes all of those letters, roman, italic, and script, which have a pronounced variation in the weight of the strokes in the individual letters themselves. Individual members of either group do not provide a satisı factory structural contrast with one another but they do contrast with a member of the opposite group. (The principle here reminds one of the taboos of primitive peoples which forbid marriage with a member of the same totem group.)

The chief use of structural contrast is to emphasize an initial of a word or a name, or to emphasize a word in a line, or to add to the contrast between a heading and the text. While it is an effective device in itself, its effect is enhanced if it is reı inforced with a contrast of weight, size, or colour.

Structural contrast is simple to devise, and requires no more experience than that which enables one to classify any type face in one of the two groups: in other words, the ability to tell the difference between thick-and-thin and a monotone type. And precisely because the contrasting groups are limited to two, each containing a vast array of different type faces, the number of potential combinations – if a designer has all the type he wants at his fingertips – is both staggering and inspiring.

Starting from a single letter of the sans serif family, we may skim over the surface of members of the other group which will contrast with it: the roman or italic of all the classic faces, Caslon, Garamond, Scotch, Baskerville, Bodoni, to cite a few; any thick-and-thin line script: Bank, Commercial, Brush, Trafton, Legend, etc.; and the free brush scripts.

The classic example of this type mixing, illustrated here, is that of the simple typographic title-page by Jan Tschichold, for his book *Typographische Gestaltung*. Tschichold, one of the greatest typographic masters of this century, employed three different types: a script which harmonized with a Bodoni, and a bold-face Egyptian which contrasted with both. Of course, there is more to this page than just typographic contrast: there are subtle relationships in size and in space that are the marks of a master.

There is scarcely a job that could come into a printing plant where the principle of structural contrast of type could not be employed to the advantage of the appearance of the finished product.

Jan Tschichold:

Typographische Gestaltung

Benno Schwabe & Co . Basel 1935

in the beginning was the word

H. N. WERKMAN *was a Dutch printer who used his typographic materials and various printing techniques to produce his famous 'drucksels' – little prints. This one emphasizes the nature of contrast of form.*

The ability to perceive form, or to create form where it does not already exist, is one of the dominant traits of the human mind, which the science of psychology is just beginning to analyse and understand. Why, for example, did ancient man, staring up at the sky at night, group isolated stars together into forms until the whole sky was a procession of men and animals wheeling in their nocturnal paths night after night? Why does a child see pictures of familiar things in the clouds? Why is it that the three dots in the margin of this page immediately suggest a shape to you, and the other four dots suggest another shape? Why do you not just see seven scattered dots and let it go at that? The answer lies in the tendency of the human mind to group elements into stable forms.

The whole basis of reading is, of course, this ability to recognize form, and so skilled is the human mind at remember ing forms that even a child of three years can be taught the rudiments of the abstract symbols that constitute our alphabet. At six or even earlier he can begin to recognize words, and long before he reaches maturity he can skim a line of these symbols, which are meaningless individually, and extract full meaning from them.

Form, to give it a definition, is the shape of a thing. The form of the letter 'a' is different from the form of 'b' and both are different from that of 'c' and so on. The most elementary contrast in typography is the contrast between the forms of letters; without that contrast, our alphabet would be able to convey nothing.

But when we speak of contrast of form in the context of

DESIGN WITH
type

design, we step from the elementary contrast that exists between letters of the alphabet to the contrast between different type families. At the beginning of this chapter it was noted that Bodoni and Bank Script were structurally the same, but that their *forms* were different: one is a roman letter, the other a script. This is the essence of the contrast of form – the capital against the lower case, the roman against the italic or the script, the tall condensed letter against the squat, fat one.

Just as in every other instance of contrast that has been discussed so far, there can be here no partial contrast. It is not possible to get effective contrast by setting a script letter against an italic one since their points of similarity are too many; both of them derive from the cursive (running) hand, and have the slight slope that is characteristic of handwriting. Conflict, not contrast, is the result.

When contrast of form is employed, it is often advisable to carry it through in every aspect. If Commercial Script, to give one example, is being contrasted with Bodoni, the contrast will be most effective if the script line is in upper and lower case while the Bodoni line is in capitals, so that not only the forms of the types but also the forms of the letters themselves are in contrast. If, in addition, the lower case letters of the script type are larger than the capitals of the roman type, the contrast in the other dimension – size – makes the contrast of form even more effective.

Some individual letters of some of our type families are visually interesting forms by themselves. At one time the writer had a strong predilection for the lower-case Garamond 'a'; the form of the letter is so rich in delicately balanced contours that the temptation to use it in a large size as an initial every time an opportunity presented itself could only be resisted by asking whether the device really helped to deliver the message. Often the answer in such cases is 'no', and the favourite initial has to be abandoned reluctantly for some more functional solution.

Other designers are attracted to the contour of a well-designed lower case 'g', and even the rigidity and direct statement of the lower case Futura 't' can exercise a fascination. These are per sonal enthusiasms which a designer can enjoy if he does not let them get in the way of the job he has to do. He must also guard against indulging pet mannerisms to the point where both his client and his audience become unresponsive to them.

This principle of contrast in the forms of letters can be applied universally. It is seen in the italicized word in a line of text, by which emphasis is achieved in a quiet way. It is also apparent in the simple relationship between a heading and the text. Monotony is avoided when the type of the heading is in complete contrast to the type of the body of the text. It reaches the extreme in the over-size display letter which possesses a striking form of its own, poised against a mass of type of a contrasting form. In business letterheads, contrast of form will often rescue the appearance from dullness and monotony; the contrast can be injected through the use of a contrasting initial, by contrasting one word of the firm name with the rest of the name, or by setting the whole name of the firm in a type which is in contrast to the informational material – address, telephone number, etc. But, in every case, to be both striking and pleasant, the contrast should be strong: two completely dissimilar and opposed faces should be fused into a unity of opposites.

A designer should cultivate an awareness of the variety of forms. available in type, and be alert to recognize when the copy presents an opportunity to use it effectively. He will thus avoid monotony in his typography, and at the same time help the reader to grasp the meaning of the message.

An announcement by BOB GILL *plays with the free forms of the lower case 'g', and contrasts them against the rigidity of a small line of sans serif text. Below,* BEV LEECH, *student at the Vancouver School of Art, contrasts structures to wittily explain a printing term.*

WRONG FOUNT

Stupid
Clod
!!!

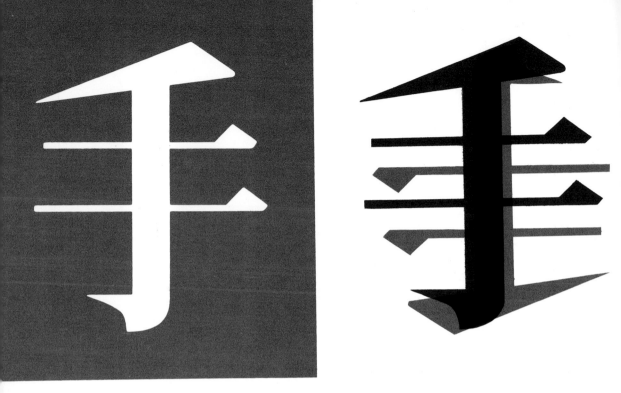

HIDEO SAITO *of Tokyo plays with Japanese characters to create new symbolic meanings. He explains the ones shown in this way: 'At upper left is the character for "hand"; beside it is a character I call "thoughtful hands", for clasping one's hands with fingers intertwined and thumbs together, elbows bent and the hands folded upward, is a common attitude indicating contemplation. The one at right I have labelled "large hands". It is meant to convey two hands with the ends of the fingers touching – the position in which one receives or lifts or carries a large object.'*

It is significant that the first printed book, the Gutenberg Bible, provided rectangular spaces at the beginning of each chapter for the insertion by hand of coloured and ornamented initials; the second book, the Mainz Psalter, had these initials printed in red or blue. This tradition of employing colour as a contrast on the printed page was carried forward from the manuscript into printing, from the hand-made book into the machine-made product.

Unfortunately, the economy of modern book production does not often allow the use of colour in books except for special editions, and then it is usually restricted to title pages and an opening initial. Children's books are an exception. Extravagance of colour and illustration is generally considered an integral part of children's publications. With some trade books the elegance and luxury of colour in the introductory pages will be considered necessary despite the additional cost. Where additional colour is used to enliven or illustrate a book from cover to cover, careful planning is essential to obtain the greatest effect at the least increase in cost. In this connection it might be appropriate to mention that the second colour in this book is the result of such planning. The two-colour pages were all run together as a 32-page unit, then cut apart and distributed through the book with the normal black and white pages.

The designer should familiarize himself with the methods used by printers in making up signatures of 16, 32, or 64 pages. He should discover how, by inserts into these signatures or by 'wrap-arounds', the visual excitement of the book can be en

hanced with no great addition to the cost. By knowing these techniques, the designer can assist his client in organizing his material for maximum effect.

In general commercial printing and advertising the use of a second colour can be visually stimulating and thus increase the effectiveness of the message. But its use is a special challenge: to make sure that the extra run on the press that is required results in a positive contribution to the appearance of the entire finished piece and thus to the dramatization of the message. It is not enough just to decide to run a heading in colour and let it go at that; the designer must have in mind the specific colour to be used and the effect he desires to create with it.

The whole subject of colour is too vast to be covered in this book, let alone this chapter, but several fundamental things can be said to clarify what is involved in making the best use of a second colour in a printing job.

First, let us examine the question of effective and ineffective colours. Colours fall into two broad classes, cold and warm. The cold colours are at the green-blue end of the spectrum; the warm colours are at the red-yellow end. The cold colours tend to recede from the spectator, the warm colours to move toward him. Obviously, then, the warmest colour should have the strongest attraction for the eye, and certainly this is true, for a brilliant orange-red is by far the most vigorous colour with black ink and white paper. But while orange-red is the most compelling to the eye, it is not always the psychologically correct colour to use. What a misuse of colour it would be to use a red-yellow-orange in a piece of advertising for an air-conditioning system!

This brings us to the second point: the contrasting relation-ships of colours. It takes only a small area of red to flame forth from the page and capture the reader's eye, but because of its tendency to recede, a large area of a cold colour is needed to make the reader realize that colour is being used. A single

A title page by HERMANN ZAPF *of Frankfurt showing this designer's mastery of typography of a monumental quality, and especially his discreet handling of colour. (From* Typographic Variations *by Hermann Zapf, Museum Books, New York.)*

The Comedies and Tragedies of William Shakespeare Complete and unabridged with notes and glossary * Illustrated by Fritz Kredel * Volume II Random House

annual histadrut dinner

At left, two colours are interwoven to make a rich texture for an invitation to dinner. Below, a cover of a book designed by EL LISSITSKY employs dramatic contrast of both colour and the forms of the letters.

display word or line on a printed job, if run in these colours, will appear lighter and more distant than the remainder of the type appearing in black. Thus the colour has not been used to advantage since it has not drawn the viewer's attention. Getting around the difficulty might involve the use of larger areas of colour, even to the point where the whole background becomes the colour.

In any case, it should be established as a principle that, no matter what colour is being used, the coloured areas and the black and white areas should never be in perfect balance. Either one or the other should be substantially greater. For the warm colours a small, discreet area is sufficient, but for the sharpest visual impact the colour must dominate; in the case of the cold colours, the coloured areas are more effective if they are larger than the black and white.

The massing of colour elements is also important. It will be an anaemic design if little bits of colour are spotted across the sheet of paper as though some dispirited house painter had wandered about slopping over drops of paint as he went. This comment infringes on a later chapter on integration, but here it needs to be said that the organization of colour in a few potent spots is the only effective way of handling it. When a solid-colour background is used, some white mass should be

Four examples of the use of colour to increase the effectiveness of a message: below, a book title (France); at right, a small ad for a German printer, in which a letter in colour frames the information; bottom left, a cover of a booklet for Cooper Union in New York; and right, below, an inscriptional page by HORST ERICH WOLTER, Leipzig.

INVASIONINVASIOIINVASION
ASIONINVASIONINASION
VASIONINVASIONINVASION
VASION INVASION IVASION 14
NVASIONINVASIOIINVASION

unsere schriften
neue offizin stuttgart
offsetdruck
buchdruck
telefon 65847

ART
Professions
in the U.S.

the cooper union

SOLI DEO GLORIA

Fest allezeit
in Freud
und Leid

Arbeit ist des
Bürgers Zierde, Segen ist der Mühe Preis

let through and countered vigorously with either a black type mass or a black area with reverse type. It is most important in using this technique that the colour used be of medium strength, so that both black and white will show up against it. There is nothing more likely to discourage a reader than being required to decipher black type against a background that is too dark. Properly applied, these simple relationships of colour, white, and black provide the most dramatic way of using colour in printing.

There are times, as was mentioned in a previous chapter, when a very soft colour is needed to shade off the mass of a huge initial, for example on a letterhead. Here is where the pure colours are often too harsh (except for yellow) and the grayed-down tones of pastel shades are preferable. The swatch book of any ink manufacturer, if thumbed through slowly and with attention to the quality of each individual colour, will suggest dozens of unusual shades which can be employed to good effect.

The use of a second colour for contrast can often make a printed job much more effective, and it may be false economy for an advertiser to restrict his printer to a single colour. Since two-colour printing can be profitable to the printer, he would do both himself and his client a favour if he did his utmost to sell the second colour whenever appropriate; such selling will be easier, of course, if it is obvious that his designer knows how to use colours effectively and to get full value for the extra cost.

It is not every customer's budget that can make use of a second colour, however effectively it is chosen. But where the budget does restrict the printing to one colour why is that one colour almost invariably black? Why not a rich, deep gray, or a dark red, or green, or brown? The colour of the ink may be contrasted against either white or coloured paper, and the printed piece will thus acquire an individuality, a visual appeal which distinguishes it from the run of mill.

contrast of direction

A human being orients himself in vertical and horizontal terms; he is vertical in his waking hours, horizontal in sleep; he orients himself by the horizon (hence the word 'horizontal'), and the things he erects on the earth's surface are true verticals established by a plumb-line. This being the established order of things, he is disturbed by anything which does not conform to it. He has a sense of insecurity when he looks at the Tower of Pisa. Conversely, when he himself is in an off-vertical position in the seat of a climbing train, the telephone poles that pass him, in the frame of his tilted window, appear to be leaning forward – surely not he, but the outside world, has tipped dangerously!

To a lesser degree, the human sense of balance is disturbed by slanted lines of type or typographic elements; but a real focal point can be created by a direct, ninety-degree angle of intersection of two typographic units. Fortunately for the typo graphic designer, his material lends itself readily to such vertical and horizontal contrasts; all typesetting is based on rectangular units. But this does not give blanket endorsement for all pos sible arrangements, such as piling individual letters of a line one above the other, or turning type on its side to make it run up or down. The former is a typographic taboo, since it makes a text illegible; the latter requires the exercise of discretion. No line of type which is of vital importance to the total message should ever be turned to run against the grain of reading habits unless it is strongly dominant and legible. Yet there are often cases when there is an obviously dominant main heading or title and a very subordinate piece of copy which could be

FRANCO GRIGNANI *of Milan constructs a full-page magazine advertisement for a printer around a massive capital 'A' with its base tilted, and with the text run in the normally slanted right-hand stroke of the letter.*

Alfieri & Lacroix, nata con l'ausilio meccanico del secolo, oggi, dopo oltre assant'anni di evoluzione tecnica e di rinnovamento, per prima in Italia si apre alle nuove estetiche grafiche. Organicamente completa in ogni settore produttivo: zincografia, tipografia, litografia, legatoria, rappresenta per il difficile mondo pubblicitario un grande e sicuro aiuto.

run vertically and make an effective contrast, but which would not affect the total meaning if it chanced not to be read.

At the point of intersection of two type rules there is a powerful field of attraction that might be compared to a magnetic field. A type composition built around such a point of conflict holds together more effectively as a unit than one which uses the more conventional border to wall in the message and confine it within a typographic cell. There should be no equality between the intersecting rules, either in their thickness or in the areas they define; intersecting rules create four rectangles of space– none of these rectangles should be the same size or shape as any other.

So much for rules and lines of type; what about areas of text matter? We have seen in the discussion on texture that strong horizontal patterns can be created in body type by employing leading. Vertical patterns can also be created, by setting the body copy on a narrow measure and by justifying the line on either the right or the left side. The alignment which this justification will create, plus the vertical nature of the narrow column, will overcome the natural horizontal movement of type and create a visual vertical thrust. Intersect this thrust at any point with a strong horizontal title line, and the type elements will be in visual collision at the point of intersection. Similarly, two masses of body type, either on the same page or on facing pages of a spread, can be made to move in opposite directions by the creation of one vertical column as described above, and one mass in which the horizontal movement is emphasized by heavy leading. Even though there is no actual point of intersection between these two, the direction of movement of the two type masses is in contrast, and a point of tension is established.

The applications of this principle are numerous; perhaps two examples will serve to illustrate the point. If a letterhead is being designed in which a long company name and a group of

A ninety-degree angle intersection, with the whole composition turned on its point, enables the 'N' and 'Z' of the Swiss daily newspaper National Zeitung *to act interchangeably. Designed by* GERSTNER+KUTTER *of Basle.*

elio vincelli

architect = architecte

429 JEAN TALON OUEST, MONTRÉAL, QUÉBEC   TÉLÉPHONE TALON 5366

short pieces of information must be used, the company name may be spread horizontally across the sheet, while the short items are set flush left to form a vertical column which intersects the main line. In a booklet or publication in which vertical columns of type dominate, the intrusion of a strong horizontal line of display sets up a visual tension in the page or spread.

There is one important point to remember when contrasting vertical and horizontal elements: because of its physical structure our eye is capable of greater movement in a lateral direction than in a vertical, and we are prone to misjudge heights in relation to horizontal distances; a vertical line will always look longer than a horizontal one of equal length. Designers have frequently used this accepted fact to increase the effect of small newspaper advertisements by running a strong vertical rule up the side. Whenever there is a dominant vertical or horizontal element in any given rectangular area, either dimension, width or height, can be accentuated through the use of opposition in direction.

Texture, to recall the discussion on the subject in chapters 5 and 6, is the pattern created by the repetition of certain chaꞁ racteristics inherent in the individual letters of a type face. Texture can therefore only exist in a line or a mass, wherever there are enough letters in an area for a textural pattern to take form. Textural contrasts involve the interplay of two other contrasts – those of structure and those of weight. The structure of the letter determines the kind of texture; the weight deterꞁ mines the relative coarseness of the 'weave'. Both of these characteristics can be emphasized or mitigated by the use of leading between the lines if the texture results from the types being viewed as a mass rather than as a series of lines.

In discussing colour, we used the terms warm and cold to describe the range of our emotional reactions to it; in the case of texture, the terms hard and soft might be applied with equal validity. A line of sans serif capitals is hard and dispassionate; text set in Garamond italic is soft and friendly to the eye. Here, then, is the basis for the play of textural contrasts in typoꞁ graphic design. In a sense, the typographer meets the same challenge as the contemporary architect; the latter, too, tries to play off textural effects, one against the other: he contrasts the warmth of wood with the coldness of stone, and relieves the varying roughness and irregularity of both of them with the smoothness and transparency of glass. But the range of textures at his disposal in building materials is very limited.

The designer of printing has a wider range of textures at his disposal, and a greater degree of control over each individual texture, since he can influence it by letting in white, either in

the line by letter-spacing, or in the mass by leading. Of course to be able to use texture with confidence the typographer should be familiar with the textural values of the type faces at his disposal. Specimen settings of a wide range of type faces appear on pages 38 and 39; each should be studied closely in relation to other faces to discover its particular textural quali ties. Adjoining settings show the same type faces with leading between the lines; they should be compared with the solid settings so that the change in textural effect brought about by the introduction of leading will be clearly understood and it will be possible to conjure up mental pictures of any type tex ture, either solid or leaded.

But what of the texture of the display line itself? Here the letters have more individuality, and they assert it more strongly because of their greater size and because they are comparatively isolated in the white space with which they are, or should be, surrounded. The texture of the display line is emphasized in the same way that the pattern of a woven cloth would be emphasized if it were viewed under a magnifying glass. A certain quality of unity may, of course, be sacrificed when the detail is enlarged. Because the detail – the structural charac teristics – is more in evidence, any changes created by letter-spacing will be correspondingly magnified.

The examples shown in the margin will demonstrate this point better than any verbal description could do. The solid line of Futura Ultrabold, for example, has the strength of a solid black bar; with adequate letter-spacing inserted, however, it becomes a series of staccato points which leads the eye along it in the same way as a dotted line.

Or again, consider a condensed Gothic letter: the solid line has a geometric unity that almost overpowers the vertical character of the condensed letter; if the line is letter-spaced, however, the vertical character of the letter dominates, and the line becomes a series of upright elements.

Opposite page: an exercise by a student required to cut up letters of a given type face to destroy recognition, and reassemble them into a texture. A contrasting type is superimposed.

DESIGN FOR GREATER

DESIGN FOR S

READY-TO-ASSEMBLE FUR

READY-TO-ASSE

SALE OF FINE LI

FINE LINE

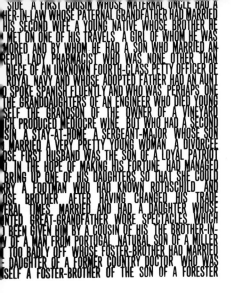

A page of text with a monotonous texture done by
MASSIN *in Paris to represent a dreary cataloguing of*
family relationships in a monologue by a character in
Ionesco's La Cantatrice Chauve.
(See also pp. 148–152.)

From the foregoing it might be assumed that the only textural contrasts possible are those involving masses of type. But it should not be overlooked that two display lines in themselves can have different textures; that even a word itself may be sufficient, if the type is well chosen, to create a texture which contrasts with its surroundings. Thus textural relations can be employed within a heading alone to create visually stimulating contrasts between the hard and the soft, the rough and the smooth, the tweeds and the silks of typography.

Once the nature of the texture of the display line has been established, whether solid or letter-spaced, the textural quality of the text matter can be designed as its decisive opposite. If the display line is letter-spaced to create a series of vertical elements, the text may be given ample leading and develop a horizontal pattern for contrast. If the display line is solid, the body type may ease off into staggered lines which defy the rigidity of its caption.

In designing books, on the other hand, the designer will start with the text and consider what is appropriate for it. He will use display as a counterpoint in preliminary pages and in chapter heads.

The potential combinations of textural qualities are only limited by the number of type faces which stand in contrast to one another, multiplied by the different effects that can be achieved through varying their texture. The range challenges the imagination and the creative instincts of the printer and designer.

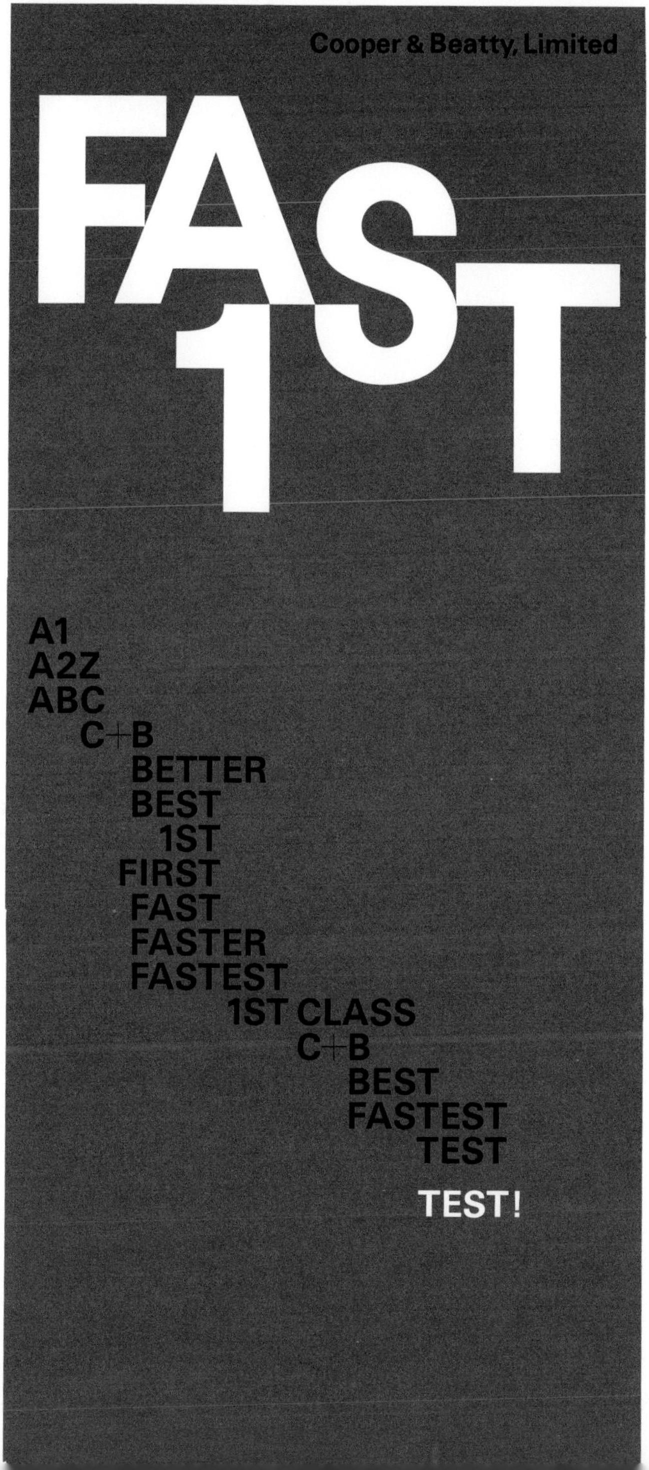

Cooper & Beatty, Limited

FAST
1ST

A1
A2Z
ABC
C+B
BETTER
BEST
1ST
FIRST
FAST
FASTER
FASTEST
1ST CLASS
C+B
BEST
FASTEST
TEST

TEST!

A cinematic handling of type in a promotion for a typesetting house, Cooper & Beatty Ltd., by ANTHONY MANN, *Toronto.*

SIZE

DIRECTION

form

texture
texture
texture
texture
texture
texture

colour

structure

WEIGHT

The seven basic contrasts which are possible with typographic material have already been compared to the notes of the musical scale; if a designer knows how to use them, he can create music. The comparison is not as fanciful as it may sound, for the effective use of typographical contrasts depends on the ability to strike chords. Individually the contrasts are perhaps visually interesting, but in combination they achieve heightened effects. Most basic contrasts need other contrasts to reinforce them; for example, contrast of size alone does not have the visual vigour of a combination which includes contrasts of form and weight.

Hmne pobnioe nimhovinp ehot obap entporhia anmnovih phoamehlmiv al pob hmnepob nioemin hovi penotob orhia amnovih pho amehlmiva bo ne minhovi ponotob apoh aoemnlipan i

The latter example is cited at random; the permutations and combinations possible with the seven basic contrasts and an adequate range of type faces at his disposal give to the designer as wide a range of effects as the musical composer has at hand. But just as every musical score has its home key, in typography the contrast of size of the typographic elements is almost a prerequisite for all other contrasts. A strong contrast in the size of the elements is basic, and all other contrasts are extra effects introduced into the relationship.

It would be impossible to explore all the potential combinations in a lifetime. Each printer or designer, within the range of type styles and sizes at his disposal, will constantly find new and exciting combinations if he is looking for them. That, of course, is the crux of the problem; no amount of perusing sheets of type specimens will ever teach a designer to recognize his opportunity, or even to recognize what has made an effective contrast in a specimen of another's work. A sharpening

The Interplayers:
A PHŒNIX
TOO FREQUENT
by Christopher Fry

Colour is handled discreetly in this handsome small folder announcing a theatrical play, designed by ADRIAN WILSON, *San Francisco.*

Below, a typographical design by IMRE REINER *of Switzerland brings all the contrasts into play in a simple statement. The elements are in total contrast: size, weight, structure, form, colour, texture, and direction. At right, square format business card by* KLAUS BURKHARDT *of Stuttgart, with many contrasts employed.*

of his own visual faculties and his habits of perception will enable him to take a typescript, search out the core of the message, and give it visual expression through typography.

How can perception be trained? One means of stimulating ideas about the application of contrast in the average commercial printing job is the study of examples of typographic design shown in graphic exhibitions. Analysis of these at every opportunity will help the printer and designer to analyse any of his own jobs and learn what will make the result effective.

Exhibitions, of course, present the work of the most highly skilled and imaginative designers, usually working with a wide range of type faces and materials and, in many cases, a generous budget. Many printers and designers have to substitute ingenuity for money and work within the limitations of their own typographic resources. However slender these resources may be, the material of contrast exists in every printing establish

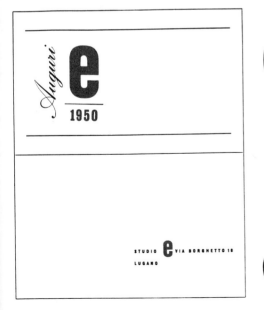

ment; the meanest shop will have more than one size of type, most shops will have more than one type face which, if they have been purchased carefully, will provide contrast.

Printers' rules by themselves can provide typographic emphasis; a skilful compositor can construct oversize initials, background areas, structural divisions, and even stylized pictorial representations with plain rules. A few strips of metal rule, some large type-high squares, a fine file, and a pen-knife can become the raw material for contrasts if used with imagination and taste.

Finally, every printer has the contrast of the texture of his type and the texture and colour of his paper; if there is nothing more than this, good typesetting in a rectangle of interesting proportions placed on the page in an unusual way that will take the greatest advantage of the interplay of paper and type can in itself be visually exciting.

Initials made up of type rules: above, the designer's monogram by SAM SMART, *Toronto; centre, monogram of letters 'as'; bottom, the author's monogram CD, a simple typographic spot with a centre bar removed.*

At left, an exercise in contrasts done as an abstract typographical 'painting' and executed for the author by students at L'Ecole des Arts Graphiques, Montreal, under the supervision of ARTHUR GLADU *in 1947.*

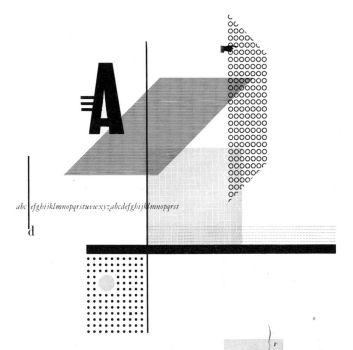

a

A blank sheet of paper lying before the designer, defying him to make something out of it, is a space. Space is meaningless until something happens in it; anyone who has travelled through prairie country will vouch for the monotony of unbroken expanses of flat land stretching to the horizon; the most welcome sight is a tree.

Why? A tree serves to interrupt the space and give it meaning; there is a point of reference for the spectator; he is able to establish relative position in space by reference to the tree; the space has been 'articulated' by a division created in it.

The articulation of space is important to the human being from infancy. At first he lives in a void, conscious, perhaps, of no more than the weight of his own body on his back. But as the eyes develop, he is attracted by a bright object dangled before him; the space he inhabits has been given its first meaning. Before long he will try with clutching fingers to reach this object, but his knowledge of space is still so limited that he will not succeed. From here on, his efforts will be directed towards the conquest of space, towards the co-ordination of eye and muscle in traversing the little world that surrounds him. As his world enlarges from his crib to the objects beyond, to the whole room, to the house, and then to the outdoors which is in his immediate neighbourhood, he is constantly learning more about the space in which he moves, and new muscles are being brought into co-ordination. From reaching for things with his arm he progresses to an attempt to move himself toward them, and he learns to crawl, to walk, and then to run, in order to conquer the space between himself and an external object in the shortest possible time.

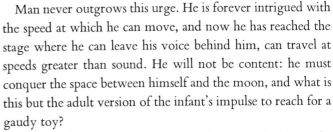

Man never outgrows this urge. He is forever intrigued with the speed at which he can move, and now he has reached the stage where he can leave his voice behind him, can travel at speeds greater than sound. He will not be content: he must conquer the space between himself and the moon, and what is this but the adult version of the infant's impulse to reach for a gaudy toy?

The visual conquest of space involves two functions, the perception of distance and the recognition of size, and the two functions are closely interrelated. To go back for a moment to the illustration of the space on the prairies: suppose, on this unarticulated plane, we were to see an object which resembled no object we had ever seen before. Lacking experience of its size, we would have difficulty in estimating its distance from us. But suppose now a second object were there, the tree of our previous example. Then the relative size of the new object and its distance from us could be determined in relation to the tree with which we were familiar. The new object would then appear near or far, large or small, in relation to the object with which we had had experience.

But sometimes the most familiar objects change their size, depending upon their direction from our normal line of vision. The moon, for example, appears larger when it is near the horizon than when it is overhead; similarly, a skyscraper looks taller in its vertical dimension that it would in a horizontal dimension along the street. As was pointed out in the chapter on contrast of direction, we overestimate vertical distances.

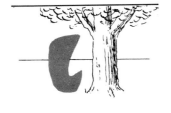

By and large, then, our judgment of distance is based on two factors: the size and position of a familiar object in relation to the horizon, and the relation of this object to other objects which stand in front of or behind it. As the distance between object and viewer increases, the object appears to diminish in size and to approach the horizon. If two objects occupy the same portion of a field, the one which overlaps the other is regarded as the nearer.

So familiar have we become with making judgments in these matters of space, that we do not think very much about it. In an automobile, we judge the distance of another vehicle moving towards us, unconsciously computing not only the space but the time involved in the approach of the two vehicles, and then we decide whether we can swing out and pass the car in front of us and return to our own lane before the oncoming car has met us. Such judgments are fortunately almost always accurate.

Up to this point, of course, we have been discussing three-dimensional space, and the reader may well be pardoned if he fails to see what connection this has with the surface of white paper which lies in front of the designer, a space which has length and breadth, but not depth. The difficulty lies in trans lating visual space into relations on a plane. A similar problem has been solved many times by painters. The Renaissance artist succeeded in creating the illusion of depth on the two-dimen sional surface of his canvas by the technique of using con verging lines of perspective. Painters before the Renaissance had achieved depth by relating the size, clearness, and position on the canvas of the elements of the painting. The Oriental painter succeeded in giving depth to his work by placing the receding planes of his picture one above the other.

What can the typographical designer do to articulate the two-dimensional space in which he has to work? Printers for years have had one stock trick for creating such an illusion: the shadow-box which appears to come out of the paper or recede into it, and sometimes to do both alternately, depending on how it is looked at. But the creation of a shadow edge is not the most important thing that happens when we look into space. More important is our discernment of relative position and size. When we see one object in space partly concealed by

The illusion of emerging rectangles is achieved by the French painter VICTOR VASARELY *in this canvas, 'Bora'. This could be set in type metal as easily as it can be done on canvas – if the creative ability is there.*

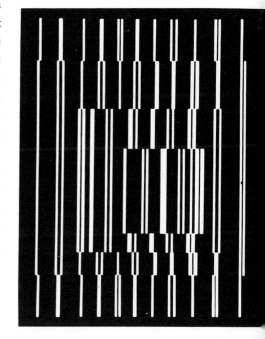

The illusion of space resulting from a double impression was used by the apprentices at the University of Toronto Press for the title page of a project done under the direction of HAROLD KURSCHENSKA.

MANIA
MANIA
MANIA
MANIA
MANIA
MANIA
MANIA
MANIA
MANIA
MANIA
MANIA MANIA
MANIA MANIA
MANIA MANIA MANIA MANIA TYPOMANIA MANIA
MANIA MANIA
MANIA MANIA
MANIA MANIA
MANIA
MANIA
MANIA

another, we know the latter is in front of the former. When this phenomenon occurs on a two-dimensional surface, the relative positions of the two objects are given a spatial connota tion. Intellectually we are aware that the two shapes in the margin of this page are on the same surface and that there is no space between them; but visual experience leads us to infer the existence of a space between them. The triangle, we insist, is in front of the circle. In the second illustration we know that there is no straight line behind the circle, that what we are actually looking at is an area of ink lying on a flat of sheet of paper, the shape being that of a circle which has a line on either side of it. But our spatial experiences dominate our intel lectual processes, and we 'see' a line which disappears behind the circle.

These are elementary spatial relationships of a three-dimen sional nature on a two-dimensional surface; they have a very direct bearing on the spatial relationships we can create with typographic material.

The principles involved can be stated quite simply: changes in size, overlapping of areas, changes of colour relationships, any variation in the treatment of the paper surface, will be invested by the eye with spatial significance. Our typographic planes can be made to appear to be nearer to or farther away from the reader.

There is no blanket prescription for achieving these impres sions, no pat formula for generating three-dimensional effects. The whole concept of space in depth on the surface of paper, using typographic material, is just beginning to be explored. Out of the daily work in printing plants will constantly come new answers for those of the trade who are looking for spatial effects. Sometimes accidents arising from effects of double im pressions, or other incidents that are routine experiences in a printing plant, will give rise to new approaches if someone with open eyes and mind will see and study them.

In the enthusiasm of discovering how three-dimensional effects can be achieved typographically, the designer must not over look the fact that the layout sheet in front of him insists that he has a two-dimensional surface to organize. He can, of course, organize this surface the way even a pigsty is organized – by putting a fence around it. This is very effective in keeping what's inside, inside, and keeping what's outside where it belongs. Typographically, it is called a border. Within this containing outline it would be possible simply to put letters and words at random and the space would certainly be articu lated. But it is a question whether those letters and words would fully succeed in performing their primary function of transmitting a verbal message. An honest printer and craftsman really has no tolerance for 'pigsty' typography; his own self-respect at the very least would make him want to tidy up his work.

Determining ahead of time how this tidiness is going to be effected involves an understanding of the way a two-dimen sional space like the surface of paper can be organized for visual attractiveness and unity. It may be granted that the verbal message of an advertisement is perhaps most important in the creation of the impulse to buy. No amount of good typo graphic design can make up for a dull and uninspired piece of copy-writing. But on the other hand the zest of a good piece of copy can be neutralized by bad typography. In the same way, a great work of literature can be rendered tedious by careless or indifferent treatment of the type pages.

If we are to discuss the means of typographic presentation

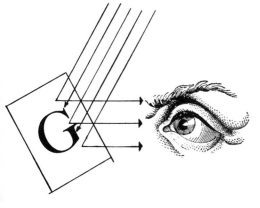

intelligently, it is necessary to take a short side excursion into the fields of optics and psychology. Let us start, then, with the reading process. The page which you are now scanning is a white sheet of paper with a multitude of black characters on it. For you to see it, there must first of all be light; the light must fall on the paper and be reflected back to the eye from the white portions and absorbed by the dark. When we read, what we really see, then, is not the printed type, but the paper itself. The type has only a negative value; we are aware of it only because it represents an area of the sheet from which no light is reflected; we do not really 'see' it.

The eye is constructed of millions of light-sensitive nerve-ends (rods and cones) which are activated when light strikes them; they carry this multitude of stimuli to the brain, and the brain organizes the light-impressions into patterns which are accepted as stable forms that may or may not be familiar. The fact that the organization of form takes place in the brain and not in the eye is an important addition to our knowledge of visual processes for which a group of psychologists referred to as the Gestalt school is responsible. (*Gestalt* is a German word meaning 'form'.) Several examples of the importance of this cerebral organization will help bring the bald scientific state ment to life in terms of the things we can readily understand.

The response to camouflage provides the best possible illus tration of the organization that takes place in the brain. An unconcealed concentration of tents where soldiers are en camped on a wooded or cultivated area of land is immediately identifiable as such from the air. The eye of the airman picks up a multitude of light impressions from the whole area, his brain organizes the pattern of dots which constitute the camp and separates it from its surroundings, and he knows his target. Camouflage prevents this organization from taking place in the brain of the observer. It attempts to blur the normally sharp definition of the camp so that its outlines cannot be

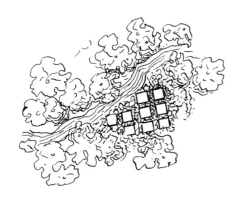

organized into a single unit. The lines of the contours of the country around the camp are repeated over and through the canvas roofs of the tents and the continuity of these lines will make the observer conclude that he is seeing country and not the shape for which he is looking.

Just the opposite of camouflage is the technique employed to help the brain organize a single unit against its background; the highway marker or the red checkered patterns that mark tall structures around an airport for recognition by aircraft are cases in point. Here the unit is made to stand out strongly against its background by contrast in pattern and colour; it is given a sharply defined shape, and the basic pattern – in many cases a checkered effect – is a stable visual unit which the brain separates immediately from the background.

Traffic lights are another instance of elements which are effec tive because of their ability to stand out in a single visual unit. Conversely, their effect is diminished when contrast is dimin ished. Many a driver has complained that on a street ablaze with red and green neon signs it is difficult to distinguish the red and green lights of traffic signals. But if a large black square is placed behind the lights to block off the flickering back ground in a definite shape, immediate organization of this space and the lone light against it takes place in the motorist's brain.

Since the first function of a piece of printing is to capture attention, design with type requires that the designer under stand how to make visual units group together for easier organization in the observer's mind. Many typographical com positions unfortunately look as though the single goal had been to try to camouflage the message– and sometimes the success is phenomenal. Camouflage in typography is simply a result of untidiness. Sharp definition requires a high degree of organi zation of the elements involved so that they will stand out as immediately as the checkerboard sign at the end of a highway.

There are established rules which can help a designer make this analysis of typographical structure, rules arrived at through experimentation with the way in which the eye receives light stimuli. They all involve the relationship between the printed area and the space which flows around and within it. The type line itself is, of course, the primary example, for the reader identifies word units by the fact that they are separated from each other by space. This is elementary spatial organization, and we have already met it in an earlier chapter. But the principles that apply for word units apply for all other units of the composition. The following discussion covers the various kinds of relationships which can be created in any given space. These relationships may be summed up as follows:

  a / proximity of units
  b / continuation of form
  c / similarity of units
  d / closure of isolated units
  e / rhythm.

a/PROXIMITY OF UNITS

It would seem almost an insult to the intelligence of the reader to state seriously as a principle of typographic design that any element has an affinity to the element or elements nearest to it. But while the principle is obvious, it is often forgotten in practice; and it is largely the failure to employ this principle that accounts for the hodge-podge of type that characterizes too much of today's typography.

Since this principle is so basic to the structure of good typographic design, it deserves close examination. In the margin is an example of seven elements, all exactly the same. In the top illustration they are disorganized; they have no more coherence than the random ink splatters made by a scratchy pen. Now examine the second example. Here an order has been created; it is possible to distinguish patterns: a unit of four elements and one of three, or a procession of two groups of three, with one element receiving emphasis because it does not conform to the pattern created by the other six. It is not diffi‍cult to see why one illustration is a confused agglomeration and the other presents stable units. The principle of proximity has been put to work to make a more acceptable arrangement; the elements have been organized through being *grouped* within a given space. Elements which are near to each other merge into a common form and are seen as a single unit. This process is the bedrock of designing with type – reducing the apparent number of elements by grouping them together into new and larger units.

Actually, the printer does this every day when he sets type. If the text of this book were to appear like the line below, even the layman would be quick to realize that the spatial organiza‍tion and the grouping of elements were wrong:

Ift het extoft hi sbookwe ret oap pearl iketh eseli nes . . .

He would object, with every justification, that the line is ille‍gible because he is forced to reorganize the elements (the letters) and the space. But the printer does not commit such atrocities; he groups the letter elements together to form words and inserts spaces between the words to give a well-defined pattern.

It is when larger units are involved that this essential typo‍graphic cohesion often breaks down, though exactly the same principle should be at work: elements must be arranged in an orderly grouping. To take a most obvious example, there must be literally millions of business cards being presented which look something like the one in the margin. Here are five elements scattered throughout the available space with precisely the same kind of visual disorganization that we had in our

MR. JOHN SMITH

representing

ALLIED MANUFACTURERS LIMITED

fabricators of steel products

1900 NORTH STREET, CENTREVILLE. XY 1234

'pied' line just above. The letters are, it is true, grouped into words, and the words into lines, but the lines fly off in all directions. The reader of this card is placed under the necessity of reorganizing the elements to gain a complete and consecu⌐tive story from the card. The words individually are holding together, which makes the task a little less onerous than in our earlier example, but they are not grouped as larger units, and the reader must therefore make a visual tour of the card to grasp all the information.

What can be done to bring order into this chaos? It will be found that units can be grouped in larger units, after a little thought to determine what things can and should be said together. Obviously, the trade mark and the name of the firm belong together: they are twin identifications that deserve association. With them belongs the identification of the pro⌐duct or service this symbol and name represent. Here, then, is one complete unit. The name of the city, the street address, and the telephone number are all items of information which tell the reader where to reach this firm; they, too, comprise a unit. The name of the representative is the main reason for the card, since its function is to introduce the man who is presenting himself on behalf of his firm; why, then, should it take a secondary position, as it does in the first example?

With this kind of planning by the typographer, the business card should begin to take a new form, as in the example in the margin. Here all the elements are organized into an orderly sequence of units of information that tells the whole story in an easy style. No other devices of typographic design, such as con⌐trasts, have been employed. This satisfactory result, achieved by the fundamental procedure of grouping material into logical visual units, is the first step in solving any typographic prob⌐lem. The same methods that have been applied to the modest business card can be used in any other situation where a number of elements of information must be presented to the reader.

b/CONTINUATION OF FORM

Continuation of form may be understood by means of an analogy with music, although the comparison may not per¬ haps be scientifically accurate. Music has different problems from those of the visual arts for the reason that its structure is built in time, rather than in space. When we listen to music, our ears are stimulated by the reception of a sequence of sound waves of varying intensity. Individually, these sounds are with¬ out meaning or interest to us; they are just isolated vibrations reaching our sense of hearing. From what, then, comes our appreciation of music?

Like our eyes, our ears relay a stimulus to the brain. It was pointed out earlier that the brain organizes visual stimuli into a pattern: the same task is performed by our auditory facul¬ ties – the brain organizes the succession of notes which we hear into a continuous form. Whether or not that organization is pleasant to our ears depends upon whether the individual notes flow smoothly from one into the other so that we can remem¬ ber them as a unit of continuous musical form. To cite extremes: there is a difference between a virtuoso at the piano and a cat walking over the keys. The catchy little tune that runs through our head all day long is a series of notes that hang together in a particularly intriguing way. It has a simple con¬ tinuity of form.

Now let us study the visual equivalent of this principle. The abstract drawing in the margin consists, as you see it, of one complete form lying on top of another, incomplete, form. But why do you not see a total shape consisting of the outline of the whole unit, with a curved line bisecting it? Or, again, why do you not see the shape at the right lying on top of the shape at the left, concealing, perhaps, a protuberance, such as indi¬ cated by the dotted line in the third sketch? The answer is, of course, that the curved line of the element on the left is a

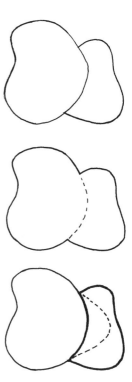

natural continuation of the other lines that circumscribe this shape; the brain follows the line of least resistance in organizing this shape, and settles on the stable form. There is a rule at work here which may be stated this way: *any line tends to be seen as continuing in its original direction.*

In terms of typographic design, the application of the rule naturally requires first of all some common line for the eye to see so that the effect of continuation will take place. This does not mean that an actual drawn line must exist. We can look at a page of type in a book and see it as a rectangle, even though there are no lines to define that rectangle; the separation between the gray mass of the type and the white of the margins defines the area as sharply as any line could do. This, then, is a typographic line, which here provides the visual boundaries of a typographic element. Now the rule can be restated in typographic terms: the visual boundaries of a type unit tend to be seen as continuing in their original directions.

Good continuation in typography simply means that these boundaries flow into one another to create a continuous form, and such a continuity serves to unify the whole composition in the same way that it provided a complete form in the first illustration in this section.

The business card on which the organization of elements was demonstrated contained also, in its reorganized form, a working example of good continuation as an integral part of its design. There is a continuous vertical axis defining the left-hand side of the lines of type, accented by the placing of the trade mark on its left.

Similarly, a line of display type straddling two pages in a title-page or a magazine spread will be seen as an optical unit despite the fact that the fold in the centre and the necessary gap of white space both act as dividing units. The directional force of the line is strong enough to overcome these breaks and create a visual unit.

There are many applications of the principle of continuation in typographic design, from the vase-shaped contours of many title-pages of classical typography, to a diagonal thrust of body type, and to the simple vertical axis and geometrical forms that are so easily adapted to the vertical-horizontal orientation of the type form.

c/SIMILARITY OF UNITS

A rule that has no exceptions is a dogma; and there are no dogmas in typography.

The law of proximity, as a prerequisite for the unification of two or more related elements, may not always be applicable. Two or more elements which are similar to each other can be employed at a distance from each other and yet give an effect of unity. As the space and the interruption by other elements increases, of course, the individual elements which are similar must be proportionately greater in strength to overcome the barriers that act to separate them.

Imagine a crowd of people all dressed in dull colours – grays, browns, dark blues. Into this blend of dark clothing and white faces come two women, widely removed in the crowd, each wearing a sweeping red hat. It is not difficult to appreciate how these two hats would create a field of visual attraction between them which would cut across the intervening crowd with a straight line and tend to unify the crowd visually.

The principle holds good in typography, too. Two typographic elements which resemble each other – in size, form, weight, colour, or structure – will create a field of attraction for each other across intervening space. If the elements are powerful enough to hold visual attention against the competition of other elements which may be interposed between them, then their attraction for each other can provide a unifying force for the entire composition.

a

A simple example of this effect, involving similarity of colour, is the practice of having one vigorous element of a letterhead (an initial or trade-mark) in a strong colour, and the signature to the letter in the same colour. The visual tie between these two areas of colour links the letter-heading to the signature, and bundles everything in between, typographic material and typewritten message, into an organic whole. Indi vidual letters, spots, rules, geometric areas of colour, the shapes contained in trade-marks and repeated with typographic ele ments – any one of these groups of elements can provide that unity through repetition at two or more points in the layout.

To grasp fully all the subtleties of similarity which can bring this effect into a composition, it is necessary also to compre hend thoroughly the characteristics of type which result in contrasts. These have been discussed in previous chapters, and if the contrasts are understood, then the similarities will explain themselves. However, a few cautions are in order.

It is important to make sure that the elements whose simi larities are to provide unity be in strong contrast to the rest of the material. Two similar elements weakly contrasting with their surroundings will never be strong enough to overpower a mass between them composed of heavier elements; a mass of text in Futura Extrabold would successfully divide two light and relatively small Caslon letters, but two Futura Extrabold letters set above and below an area of text in Caslon would be drawn to each other.

Similarly, the distance between the similarities must be sig nificant. If the two hats of the women in our analogy came together, only conflict and friction would result. If two such outstanding elements must meet, a visually more exciting effect is produced when they are dissimilar. Dissimilarity requires, of course, the contrasts we have already discussed at length.

d/CLOSURE OF UNITS

It has already been mentioned that the human mind attempts to organize unrelated units into a stable pattern; the way in which man has grouped the stars into the familiar patterns was given as an example of this form-seeking instinct. This effort to create form from isolated units is also the basis of the children's game of drawing a line through a series of numbered dots to create a picture. People enjoy the beauty of form and colour in a sunset, or in patterns on a printed fabric; they will stare with fascination at the forms that a fire in the fireplace can take. In this effort the mind is not necessarily seeking a form which recognizably relates itself to earlier experience; rather it is seeking a stable form. Having found such a form, the viewer has a sense of aesthetic pleasure. Some people are disturbed by abstract painting because they fail to recognize any familiar form when they view it, but if they will look long and recep¦tively at most abstract paintings they will have the satisfaction of a visual response to form and colour which their mind organizes into stable units, and they will then derive great pleasure from their contemplation. This approach can create a new appreciation of classic pictorial art, too. Many viewers fail to understand the form of this art, so complete is their involvement in the skill of pictorial presentation.

The organization of form from isolated units is a process that could be described as drawing a mental line to connect the points. What happens in the process is that the eye moves from one point to the other and establishes the form from the direc¦tion of its movement. The spots in the margin of this page are unconnected, but they are seen as a circle through the circular movement of the eye that encompasses them. The series of horizontal type rules are really just lines, not the triangular mass they appear to be. The process which is at work when we look at these isolated units is referred to as 'closure'. The

brain creates a form from the relative position of each unit; the form is there only because we put it there.

The creation of unified form is one of the major responsi i bilities of the typographical designer, and the principle of closure offers him the opportunity of so arranging his material that he can be sure the reader will see exactly the form he intends him to see; the unification of the composition will take place in the reader's brain along predetermined lines.

But the form the typographer aims at must be a satisfactorily stable form. It must not contain a directional movement – a linear form – that will carry the eye out of the composition as a whole. When a directional movement is created, another element must be introduced which will stop it at a certain point and hold the reader's attention within the layout. If this is not done, the directional impulse of a line may find a point for good continuation in an adjoining subject; the eye will then be carried along outside the original area, and the designer will have lost his reader.

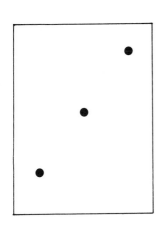

Thus three strong elements in a layout should never be grouped statically in a straight line, whether that line be hori i zontal, vertical, or diagonal, unless the line is powerfully inter i rupted. The three points, for best effect, should be distributed in such a way that they form a triangle, with none of the sides parallel to the rectangular sides of other typographic elements or to the edge of the paper.

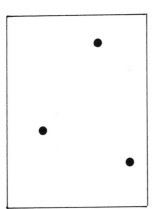

If each of the units being employed as the outside limits of a form which is to be created through closure has sufficient strength, the area over which closure can take place is as great as the area which the eye can take in. Three small similar units at the extreme edges of a full newspaper page held close to the reader will not assist closure because the eye cannot grasp the relationship over so wide an area. If the newspaper page is placed across the room from the reader, closure will take place.

In designing printed matter, the creation of a unified mass

through the association of these isolated elements is an impor‐
tant principle. Without it, the random assembly of a number
of elements would result in disorganization and confusion;
with it the designer can deliberately make the reader move
visually through the layout and create for himself a relevant
form.

e/RHYTHM

A sense of rhythm develops very quickly in people. It often
exists in a rudimentary form in an infant before he has con‐
quered space: in his rhythmic hand-clapping or leg move‐
ments, in the movements of his eye as he watches a swinging
toy. Music and dancing are further expressions of rhythm, and
the appreciation of them is common to all stages of social
development; the rich rhythms of jungle drums and the dances
that accompany them do not differ in essence from the sounds
of Western orchestras and dancing feet repeating the rhythm.

These are all rhythms that exist in time; time is divided into
precise units, not necessarily equal, but with an exact mathe‐
matical relation to each other. Typographical rhythm is no
less a rhythm because it exists only in space and is perceived
instantaneously. The regular repetition of the same form in
intervals of space is no different in essence from the regular
repetition of a musical beat at intervals in time.

Rhythm can be utilized in typography in a number of effec‐
tive ways. The regularity of letter-spacing in a line of con‐
densed capital letters creates a sense of a steady beat, each
individual letter striking its single note in space. The regularity
of intervals of space between words contains a rhythmic
quality. Typographic rules or simple geometric ornaments
repeated at uniform distances beat out a visual tattoo for the
reader. Type lines or masses similarly disposed with well-
defined intervals between them convey the same effect. And

Rhythmic repetition is a characteristic that is common to both music and electronic computers. In the upper illustration, the rhythms of Schoenberg's music as represented typographically on a book jacket by JIŘÍ RATHOUSKY *of Prague, while below the computer's rhythm is indicated in an advertisement by the Swiss designer* SIGFRIED ODERMATT.

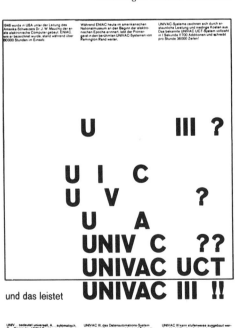

often the simple repetition of an initial, a word, or a name can remain fixed in the memory in the same way as the tricky rhythm of a popular song.

In the musical form, rhythm is not a monotonous repetition of notes at evenly spaced time intervals. Variation in the duration of the notes brings in an element of contrast, even while the basic beat remains uniform. But the accent, the grouping, provides a pattern of measured time. Similarly in typography, variations in pattern can be introduced, provided the basic measure is uniform. The established rhythm of a line of letters can be varied by the introduction of a visual 'downbeat,' by an accented letter which, by its size or weight or colour, varies the steady beat while still maintaining the spatial rhythm. But the regular rhythm must be well established for the accent to have effect. Typographic rhythm, whether it is achieved by way of the initials or the name of a product, a firm, or a trademark, can provide interesting backgrounds or borders for covers, packages, labels, or advertisements. Repetition is the essence of rhythm, and repetition can be of great importance in emphasizing a name which the advertiser is anxious to impress into the public mind – in fact, this is probably the origin of the term 'drumming it in'.

In books, rhythm plays a similar though often less conspicuous part. Similarities of type and spacing in successive chapter headings establish the rhythmic form, from which the structure of individual words and lines in the titles provides the variation that makes for rhythmic interest. The preliminary material must introduce this subtle and unobtrusive rhythm that will pervade the book. It must harmonize with the chapter openings and the setting of the text, while maintaining its own internal rhythm consisting of patterns, contrasts, and controlled departures from the norm. It acts to arouse and sustain the reader's interest, to set the tone of the succeeding text, and to lead him into concentration on the author's meaning.

without acknowledgment. This habit affected almost all the great scientists of the 16th and 17th centuries, whether Catholic or Protestant, and it has required the labours of a Duhem or a Thorndike or a Maier to show that their statements on matters of history cannot be accepted at their face value.

Crombie grants that some of the older science became more accessible *via* printing; but does he not simply ignore the dynamic of later medieval science towards visual formulation? For, to translate force and energy into visual graphs and experiments was, as it continued to be until the discovery of electro-magnetic waves, the heart of modern science. Today, visualization is recessive and this makes us aware of its peculiar strategies during the Renaissance.

The invention of typography confirmed and extended the new visual stress of applied knowledge, providing the first uniformly repeatable commodity, the first assembly-line, and the first mass-production.

✱ The invention of typography, as such, is an example of the application of the knowledge of traditional crafts to a special visual problem. Abbott Payson Usher devotes the tenth chapter of his *History of Mechanical Inventions* to "The Invention of Printing," saying (p. 238) that more than any other single achievement, it "marks the line of division between medieval and modern technology . . . We see here the same transfer to the field of the imagination that is clearly evident in all the work of Leonardo da Vinci." From now on "imagination" will tend more and more to refer to the powers of visualization.

The mechanization of the scribal art was probably the first reduction of any handicraft to mechanical terms. That is, it was the first translation of movement into a series of static shots or frames. Typography bears much resemblance to cinema, just as the reading of print puts the reader in the role of the movie projector. The reader moves the series of imprinted letters before him at a speed consistent with apprehending the motions of the

The frequent recurrence of a bold statement replacing chapter headings creates a rhythmic pattern through the pages of The Gutenberg Galaxy *designed by* HAROLD KURSCHENSKA

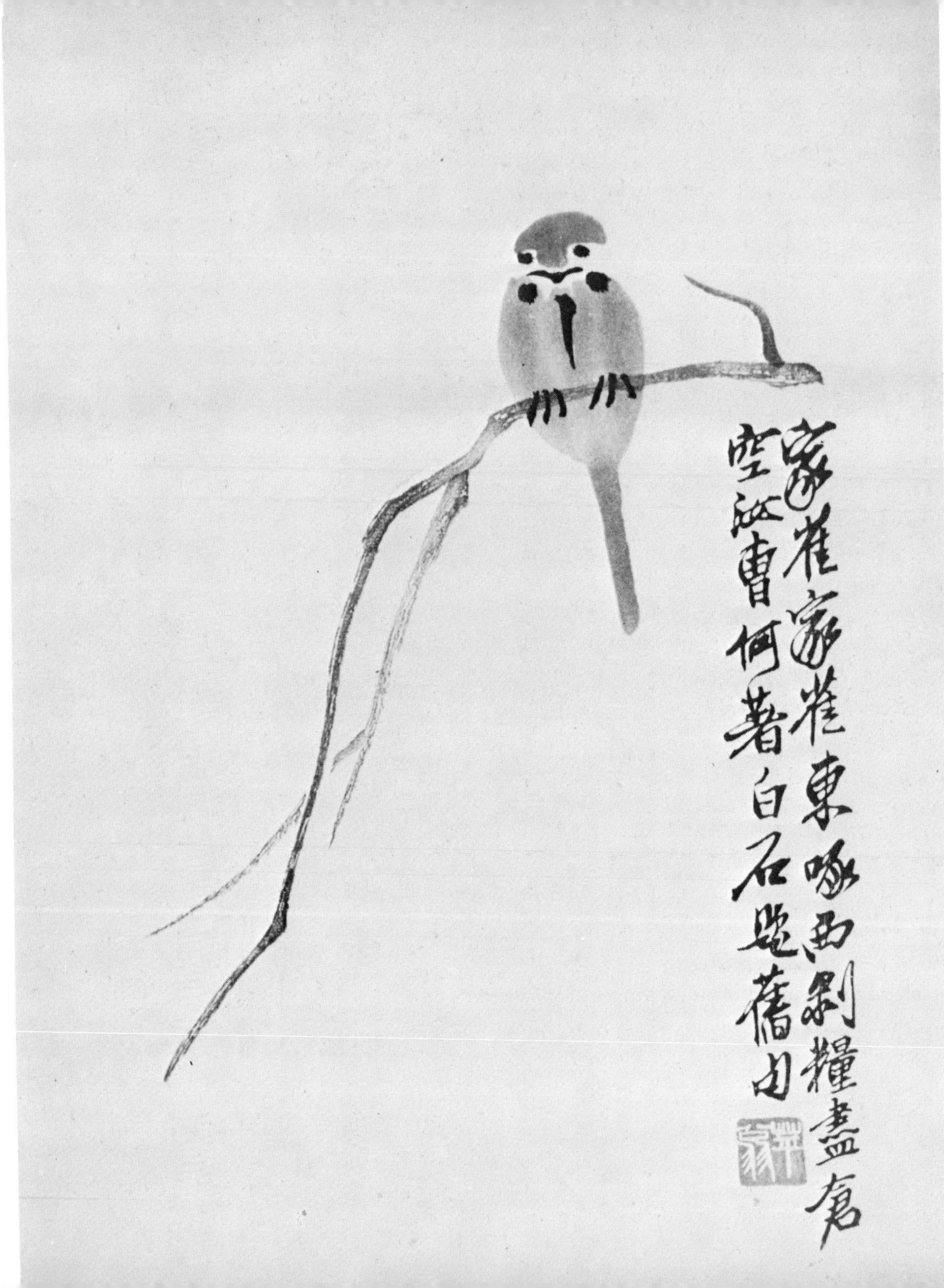

家雀家雀東啄西剝糧盡倉
空汝曹何著白石題舊句

Up to this point our attention has been directed to the study of materials. Like an architect, we now know the intrinsic charac ter and qualities of the brick and glass, the stone and wood of the typographical structure. But we have scarcely begun to build.

From here on, the challenge of typography, like the chal lenge of architecture, is the integration of the materials into a structure which will perform a desired function. The architect must delve into the activities of the people who will live or work in his building. He must organize the space at his disposal to fit those activities; he must engineer the divisions of that space for structural stability, and he must utilize his materials in an aesthetically satisfying way.

The typographer's problems run parallel to the architect's all the way. The function of the printed product he is designing is his primary consideration. Who is going to read it? Why are they going to read it? When are they going to read it? What are they expected to do when they have read it? All these questions must be answered before any truly functional design can be undertaken. There is a world of difference in the typo graphical requirements of a ticket to a ball and a catalogue of machinery parts, of a volume which is to be read in a quiet evening hour of leisure and a mailing piece which must fight with others for the attention of a possible purchaser.

The subject-matter of the printed piece will be the strongest influence on its appearance. It must look appropriate, in size, typography, colour, to the nature of the product, and to the type of person to whom it is addressed. The typography of an

Opposite page: Oriental art supplies many examples of complete integration of all elements of a painting, with the inscription as a vital part of the whole composition. In this painting the two are mutually dependent; neither could be removed without destroying the sensitive balance of the composition.

advertisement for a sophisticated beauty salon will be somewhat different from that of a direct-mail piece designed to sell farm machinery.

When a designer knows what task the printed material is expected to do, the design problem emerges and begins to dictate certain forms; and at that point the problem of engineering the structure arises.

In accordance with the laws outlined in the preceding chapters, typographic structure can be static or dynamic, passive or active. The title-page with all centered lines, suspended on a vertical axis created by the uniform projection of the type lines on either side of the centre, is typography which has come to rest; there is no movement in the composition whatever. It is static, but that is not to say the page will not be read; the static book page is quiet and demands of the reader no visual or intellectual effort to absorb the text; it invites him to sink back with the prospect of entertainment or of concentrated study without any typographic diversion.

But advertising and commercial typography must always compete for attention; they must thrust the message of the copy before the reader so that he cannot escape its impact. Active, dynamic structure is required; there must be a visual compulsion about the presentation of the message.

Dynamic layout means, invariably, an off-centre balance, an asymmetrical arrangement of the whole structure. It also requires that the number of typographical units be kept at a minimum so that there will be strong visual impact and a free, uncluttered movement of the eye through the printed area. Reducing the number of units involves the organization of the material, at the copy stage, into aggregates, each with its own form, texture, and weight. These units must then be placed in direct contrast with each other and arranged structurally on the two-dimensional surface so that they hold together as a harmonious visual unit.

Assembling the final and irreducible elements into a struc-ture that commands attention is a matter of organizing the space within the area of paper which the design is to occupy. Arrangement in an asymmetric balance challenges the inge-nuity and freshness of the typographer's imagination.

Unity of composition implies a centre of gravity and a focal point to which the eye will be drawn at once. To achieve this, one single element must dominate, and the other elements must take their position in space in relation to that point of focus. What that element is will be dictated by the nature of the copy, the purpose of the message, and the perspicacity of the designer in singling it out and giving it effective typo-graphic treatment. There are no pat answers; only creative thinking directed to the problem, backed up with a knowledge of the nature of typographic materials and the technical limita-tions of typesetting, and with an ability to organize space effectively, will give the right approach for each assignment.

A highly skilled hand may deliberately break a rule of design, may interfere with the normal optical processes and hold his reader by the visual jolt he has received. This jolt has its parallels in other phases of human experience. The early jazz bands used it in their music; the rhythm was strong and in-sistent and then suddenly it was broken – a beat was missed; there was only a silent void where the rhythm should have persisted, and then the rhythmic music carried on as though nothing had happened. The 'break' in jazz music was an auditory shock. The act of walking is a rhythmic motion, but if in preoccupation you fail to notice the curb and step off, the interruption in the rhythmic muscular movement constitutes a physical jolt. Any visual form which is incomplete challenges the reader to find the missing part and mentally return it to its place; but if this missing part is now performing a new func-tion, he must integrate the two elements to which it belongs. An example of this effect might be the dropping of a letter

A strongly framed composition by GERHARD SCHNEIDER, *student at the Werkkunstschule in Offenbach am Main. Compare with the version on page 54.*

APART

HEID

p renatal
paren tal

STE L

made in **E** ngland

EQUALITY IS
MONOTONOUS

MONOTONY
IS DEADLY

completely out of a word, leaving its position blank, and using the letter as an initial of the text, or of the signature. The misplaced letter becomes a link between the element from which it has been taken and the element with which it is newly associated.

Pattern breaks, breaks in the continuity of an otherwise stable form, incomplete closure patterns – all of these create in the reader's mind the need to restore the normal rhythm or equilibrium of solidity of form, and consequently focus his attention on the point of interruption. Printers will understand this well if they will recall how a broken leader in a long line of leaders seems in its very absence to be the most noticeable thing on the page. Or how a wrong-font letter stands out from the rest of the line because of its difference! These are, of course, accidents of the printing trade; properly controlled, what might seem errors of omission can become dynamic focal points of interest.

In any case, the aim is to create a unified effect. Unless his ability to visualize is strongly developed, a designer will find it helpful to make 'thumbnail' sketches of the layout, little miniatures done in pencil with just the major areas sketched in to indicate their approximate texture, weight, and form. Working in miniature, without concern for detail, assists the designer in keeping his composition simple and his elements compact and coherent.

The problems of relationship within the structure vary with every job, according to the kinds of visual units and their characteristics. But certain basic structural principles can be established that will apply to most problems:

1   Each of the units should be in some form of contrast to the others. Equality in the size or tonal value of the various units can create a monotonous pattern, with no one of them having predominance as a focal point in the composition. There should be a contrasting relationship of size, weight, or

direction, or better still, of all three. The principles behind the achievement of contrast have already been described fully in earlier chapters.

2   The white areas within the component parts of the layout should also stand in unequal relationships. Three units which have the same amount of white space between them will appear less interesting than they would if the spacing were varied. The units which belong together will have less space between them than a third unit which is less closely connected in meaning.

3   Marginal relationships should be unequal. The white space which frames the typographical structure is as important as the white areas within it, and unequal relationships will create strong movements within the composition. The tensions which exist between various units are all seen in the framework of the rectangular sheet of paper they occupy, and their movement towards and away from the edges of the rectangle determines the force of those tensions.

4   A directional movement should tend to originate at the edge of the sheet. To give specific examples, a vertical mass moving down into the layout should begin nearer to the top of the sheet than to any of the other sides; a horizontal area should begin nearer one side or the other, depending upon the disposition of the other units.

5   Every typographic structure should rest on a solid foundation. As with a building, the solidity of a typographic composition depends upon the firmness of its base, and all directional movements which lead down – and our reading habits will usually carry us in that direction – must have a positive terminus, whether it be a signature line, a type rule, a wide margin, or any other element that puts 'finis' to the composition.

6   The dynamic relationship between the elements must finally resolve itself into a balance. Balance is a delicate inter

inequality

TENSION

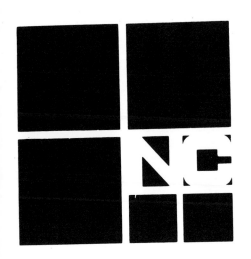

play of size and weight which defies any mathematical formu⏐lation; only the eye is capable of judging relative weight. The volume of absorbent cotton needed to balance the weight of a linotype slug is considerably greater than the volume of the metal, and the analogy applies to the visual equivalents of light grey areas of type against compact black areas. Using the optical centre of the layout as the fulcrum, the light large masses and the small heavy masses can be moved towards or away from that fulcrum in the same way as heavy and light masses must be moved towards or away from the fulcrum of a see-saw to reach a point of balance.

Dynamic, asymmetric layout requires keen judgment of the comparative values of the various elements around the fulcrum of the layout. An easier solution might be a static centring of the material on a vertical axis, but the visual appeal of the off-centre structure is so much greater that the extra effort, and the subsequent satisfaction derived from it, is worth while. When everything has fallen into place, the play of contrast of material results in a striking composition with great visual and verbal effect.

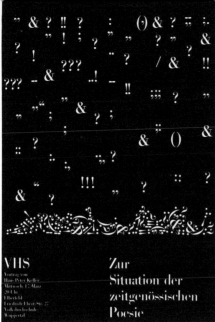

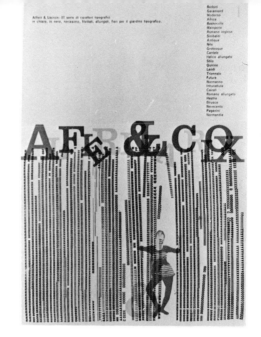

Examples of dynamic and asymmetric layouts: at far left, a trademark by NIPPON DESIGN CENTER, *Tokyo, for Nippon Cloth Industry Co.; next, an organized showing of the variations of Univers type designed by* ADRIAN FRUTIGER; *a literal 'snowfall' of punctuation creates an element of activity and motion appropriate to this advertisement for the Volkshochschule, Wuppertal, designed by* ALBRECHT ADE; *right, a newly unpacked font of type becomes a curtain for a typographic drama by* FRANCO GRIGNANI *executed for a Milan printer; below, contrasting elements and colours are employed by* HAROLD KURSCHENSKA *of Toronto for a university student publication.*

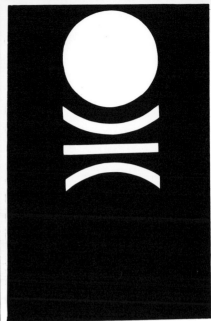

A simple typographical device links together all the aspects of the book One Chinese Moon. *Bound in black cloth with the type and symbol in white, the spine and front of the case set the pattern, which is picked up by the title page, contents page, and chapter headings. Designed by* ARNOLD ROCKMAN.

ONE

CHINESE

MOON

—

J. TUZO WILSON

FIVE

Manchurian Baedeker

On Monday, August 25th, I awakened to my first full day in China. The train was passing through the last hills of the border country. It was still cold and mist shrouded the cliffs along the narrow river valley. We cleared the last gorges and ran down broadening valleys to the swamps and plains of northern Manchuria.

The north of China is not so thickly populated, nor does it resemble the fertile plains I was to see in the south. The extensive fields were richer than those of Siberia but at first the only crop was hay.

Throughout the day it was prairie country with few trees and these for the most part looked like cottonwood. Although hot by noon in August, it was clearly a land of long bleak winters for there were numerous piles of snow fences by the railway. Strenuous efforts were being made to establish a natural snow barrier by plantations of native bushes and poplar trees for miles beside the track. I had noticed similar efforts in Siberia.

Many areas were still uncultivated and I saw one tractor which I thought was breaking virgin ground. The villages were some distance apart, but where we passed people there were many more of them than in Siberia.

Many men were working along the route laying addition-

The basic principles of typography, if they are basic and if they are principles, will apply to all forms of communication through the printed word. The emphasis in these pages so far has tended to be on the application of these principles to advertising and other display typography. Because the typography of commercial messages must be such that they are able to reach out and demand attention, with the minimum of resistance from the reader, the designer is called upon for a special effort of ingenuity and inventiveness.

Yet the designer of a book can never simply rely on traditional practices for book pages just because he has a more tractable audience. The fact that a person voluntarily picks up a book or magazine and sits down to read it does not mean that the designer's only duty is to make it legible. On the other hand, the reader of such material takes it up because he wants to be entertained or informed by the author, not diverted by the virtuosity of the designer. Thus between the two extremes of unrelieved monotony and typographical pyrotechnics there is an area where the typographic designer can contribute to the pleasure of reading and the understanding of what is being read. This chapter undertakes to discuss these facets of design.

It should be at once obvious that the chapters of this book which deal with the letter, the word, the line, and the mass establish principles which are as valid for the book as they are for the display piece. But the principles of concord and contrast, of structural and spatial relationships, are equally valid, though they may not be applied as vigorously in book work. The reader is reminded that the many details of book produc tion, which cannot be treated here, can be studied in many good reference works.

The principles of book design are not new. Mediaeval books, whether written by scribes or printed by the early printers, employed contrast of size, colour, form, texture, weight, and so on in chapter headings, initials, and margin and tail-piece decorations. These elements were not used primarily to attract attention; they were used to provide a relief for the eye, a change of pace from the fatigue of continuous reading, or just a place for the eye to come to a pleasurable pause while the mind absorbed what it had read. The mediaeval illuminators, miniature painters, and decorators knew their place and kept it. They did not try to steal attention from the contents of the book; but on the other hand their delicately ornamented pages went far to make the reading of the book a pleasurable experience, a delight to the eye as well as to the mind.

There are a few healthy signs that indicate this attitude is returning to influence the designer of the contemporary book. The problem is how to carry out these good intentions in a contemporary way. It is not enough to sift through the hellbox of typographic history for ornamental devices that pleased the eye of the sixteenth-century reader. What could be more inappropriate than one of Geoffroy Tory's criblé initials used to decorate the text of a book by James Joyce!

Yet just such outrageous juxtapositions have been perpetrated. Perhaps the trouble is that the modern designer is lazy. The printer-designer of the first few hundred years of printing designed and cut his own ornamental material in the taste of his time, and embellished his books with it. Today, it seems that only the private, limited deluxe edition has such extravagant attention lavished upon it. These editions are, however, expensive; only recently have designers begun to extend their talents and efforts to the production of books intended for a larger reading audience. Three designers have in fact made important innovations in the treatment of the modern book. Their contributions are discussed in chapter 15.

All attempts to change the conventions of book design begin with a re-evaluation of the functions of the book in our period. First and foremost of the conventions is that of the margins, which dictates that the gutter margin should be the narrowest, the head margin proportionally a bit wider, the outside margin wider still, and the bottom margin greatest of all. These clas sical margins are based on the theory that a pair of facing pages are seen as a visual unit. We might question the validity of that concept. In practice, two facing pages are read one at a time in a sequence; why then should they be paired visually? This is not to say that classical margins do not give a handsome effect, particularly when those margins are as generous, even extravagant, as were those of the fifteenth-century book. (And this, you will remember, was in a period when each sheet of paper was made by hand from pulp which contained nothing but rags! Today, when machine-made paper derived from wood pulp constitutes the bulk of our books, we are much too niggardly with our margins.)

But there is no real reason why these classical margins must be a sacred law of bookmaking today. Functional reasons may dictate other proportions; for example, pocket-size volumes which are held with the thumb of the reader in the gutter might well have a wider margin there to accommodate the thumb so that the text is not covered. Aesthetic reasons and symbolic reasons may well justify moving the rectangle of text away from its conventional position, or changing its conven tional proportions. The fundamental requirement is, of course, that the margins be of pleasing proportions in relation to each other and to the measure of the text and the page. This is a matter more of the judgment of the eye than of any precise mathematical formula.

The question of typography as an assistance in the inter

A distinguished work of typography was done for Thomas Mann's Tables of the Law *by* PAUL RAND. *The designer deliberately challenged traditional margins and formal chapter openings, and proved that a refined sense of proportion is more important than a blind acceptance of convention.*

pretation of the author's meaning is a broad one that deserves a book by itself, but must be taken up briefly here. Certainly, to take one rather obvious example, a rapport between the typographer and an experimental writer could result in the typographic form reinforcing the literary forms and meanings. No particular service is rendered to the reader by putting the new prose forms of a contemporary writer into a rigid typo graphic rectangle. *Ulysses* did not come from the same literary mould as *Uncle Tom's Cabin*; why should it be poured into the same typographic mould? The books are different; they should look different.

This approach requires a good deal of effort and imagination on the part of the book typographer; he must steep himself in the literary forms and meanings of his author. He may be obliged to design his typographic interpretation page by page, line by line. If he succeeds in making the typography part of the essential form and content of the author's words, he is improving the channel of communication between the author and reader.

Such opportunities for interpretative typography in books are, however, few and far between, and the acceptability of new forms in book design is inhibited by traditional reading habits. The designer, therefore, must concern himself primarily with the pleasant legibility of his pages, and with the freshness of his treatment of the preliminary pages, the binding, and the encasing jacket. These provide an invitation to the reader and engage his interest in what is to follow.

One of the greatest problems is to achieve a unity of design across all of these parts of a book which have such varied func tions to perform. The jacket, for example, is a pure piece of packaging, and its design should be directed toward capturing the eye and selling the book at the main point of purchase – in the bookseller's. Yet there must be a quality to the jacket which links it to the text pages and makes it at least compatible with

A playful jacket by the designer JIŘÍ RATHOUSKY *of Prague in which it is evident that the designer was interpreting the substance of the book. The original was in green and black, with the white of the basic stock showing through.*

them, if not definitely related. Each of these parts of the book becomes a challenge in itself, all of them related to the problem of expressing the theme of the book in type, colour, and design.

Jackets run the whole gamut from simple typographic arrangements to full-colour illustration. The purpose, however, is always the same; to act as a miniature poster which has to fight for attention in the colourful displays of the bookstore, and to convey an idea of the contents of the book to the buyer. The prime requisite is that it should, like a poster, convey the important information legibly and dramatically from a short distance away. Simplicity and boldness are most effective here; fussy details and timid typography defeat the purpose of a jacket. The design of the spine of the jacket is most important if it is to catch attention when the book has retired from the display rack to the shelf.

The function of the jacket is a transient one; the case serves as the permanent container of the book, and the lettering on the spine provides the identification of the book on the book shelf. The selection of the material which covers the boards, its colour, its visual and tactile properties, should relate if possible to the subject-matter. This material could even be patterned paper, with the designer using a motif based on the subject for his pattern. Photographic reproductions can also be used, on cloth or paper, whether of textures, physical features, or abstractions.

The spine should identify the book on the shelf. Unless the texture or design of the case is so unusual as to make it instantly recognizable, the visual motif should be clearly identified with the title.

The spines of books and their dust jackets often must be printed with titles that run vertically, where individual words in the title are too long for the thickness of the book. There is no real escape here, although designers may well suppress their distaste for hyphens or the breaking of words to allow some

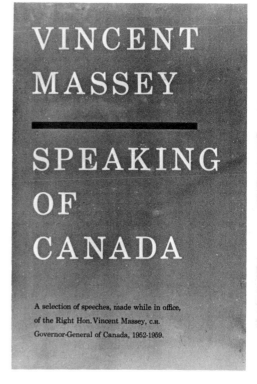

VINCENT
MASSEY

SPEAKING
OF
CANADA

A selection of speeches, made while in office, of the Right Hon. Vincent Massey, c.h. Governor-General of Canada, 1952-1959.

A simple but strong typographic jacket which states its subject with fitting clarity and dignity, by SAM SMART, *Toronto.*

solutions which rely on the spatial grouping of broken words. But where the title must be run vertically, it would be useful if some standard answer could be reached to the question whether the title should run down from the top or up to the top. At present it seems to be accepted that the title should always touch a point near the top, but designers and publishing houses vary in their preference of direction. Two functional considerations would seem to favour the convention that the title should run from the top down: first, this direction conforms to our normal reading practice of starting at the top of a page, and the top is a more natural starting point for the eye than a mid-spine position; second, when a book or group of books are lying flat, face up, a title running from top to bottom of the spine is seen right-side up, running from left to right. Vertical assembly of the letters of the title on a spine should only be used when the title consists of a single short word.

The end papers of a book have the physical function of concealing the folded-in edges of the binding cloth and the fabric which hinges the case to the bulk of the book. Most frequently, the economics of publishing dictate that the end paper should be a single sheet of blank paper. However, it can provide a visual transition from the jacket and case to the pages of the book itself. A coloured paper, or an appropriate pattern or illustration printed on the paper, can provide that visual link.

Once we are into the body of the book, certain definite relationships of the type to the page must be established and kept consistent throughout. The relationship will be determined by the size of the text page of type and its positioning on the paper page, and by the relation of margin to type area. It is not necessary that preliminary pages fill out to these margins, but they should never exceed them, and they should be laid out in the rectangle which represents the outer limits of the full text page.

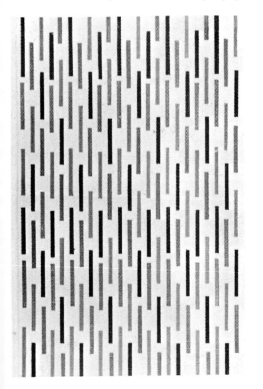

A handsome binding of white buckram which has been printed with type rules in black, green, and mauve, designed by HORST ERICH WOLTER *of Leipzig.*

The preliminaries consist of the half-title, the title page, the imprint of the printer and copyright details on the verso of the title-page, and the contents and preface and/or introduc tion, all of which should always open on right-hand pages. Just before the text there is usually a bastard title, in essence a repetition of the half-title, which separates the preliminaries from the main body of the book.

The title-page is, of course, the typographic keystone of the book; it establishes the typographic style, the mood. It is the one place in which the designer can express himself and his feelings about the book without coming between the author and the reader. It should not be flamboyant: it does not have to compete for attention. It must, however, appear as a com plete visual entity to the reader who has picked up the book and opened it. Here there can be no rules. Taste, good judg ment, a fine eye for proportion, and a discriminating use of type are the ingredients of the title page.

A table of contents is obligatory in a reference work, and of little use in a work of fiction. In many cases it is a useful guide to the prospective purchaser as to the nature and scope of a work. It should be clean and uncluttered, and should avoid the use of 'leaders', those long lines of dots that can form a pattern which appears more important than the type itself; an arrange ment of page numbers and chapter headings to meet against a vertical axis will eliminate the use of leaders without obliging the eye to search for the proper pairing.

Preface and introduction can be distinguished from the main body of the text, either by using a different size from the text or by using italics. While this is not a general practice, its effect can distinguish the typography of a book.

Throughout the preliminaries, uniform alignment of the heads of pages should be established; where these are dropped from the normal top margin they should conform with the drop of the chapter headings in the body of the book.

An effective working out of a contents page of a small anthology, requiring the listing of an author's name, the title of the story, and the page number. The page numbers provide a central axis against which the other information is placed with free outer edges. Designed by FRANK NEWFELD, *Toronto.*

CONTENTS

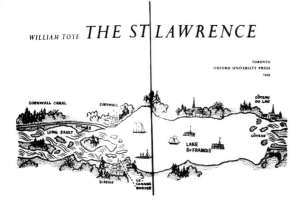

TORONTO
OXFORD UNIVERSITY PRESS
1959

Starting with the end papers, the delightfully illustrated map of the St. Lawrence River proceeds through the first thirteen pages in this book by the author-designer WILLIAM TOYE, *to provide all of the information required by the normal preliminary pages, yet weave them together in a cinematic 'panning' of the subject of the book. The illustrations are by* LEO RAMPEN.

The sequence from the half-title through to the beginning of the text, considered as a unit, offers the designer the possibility of treating the preliminaries as a sequence rather than as a series of isolated pages. The concept of extended preliminaries is a relatively new one in book design. Using different papers that progress through a series of colours, textures, or transı parencies, or using a sequence of illustrations through extended preliminaries gives the reader a cinematic effect of moving into his subject as he approaches the text pages.

The chapter heading is the last place where the designer can have his little fling. Of course here too, he must restrain himı self to a simple statement of the chapter number and title, if any. But within the space which is allowed by the drop for the chapter opening, his good taste in interpreting the author can come through. The repetition of his major motif, the use of a decorative ornament echoing his title page, the reflection of gaiety, austerity, efficiency, or whatever mood the author's work has dictated, can occur here.

In most cases the typographer will design the text page first, and all the other elements of the book will be treated as an extension of the texture established in it. This is the ultimate test of the typographer's art: the necessity to weave a page that is legible without distracting, that does a clean-cut job of comı munication while possessing a satisfying abstract texture.

Fundamental to this achievement is the choice of the type face, and the text will often help to determine this for the

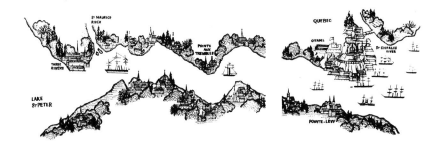

designer. This does not mean that a type face necessarily has to be 'in period'. Just because Baskerville was designed at the end of the eighteenth century does not mean that it is appropriate for a historical novel based on that period. Only the typo‐ graphic historian can appreciate such a subtlety. But types do have essential qualities, romantic, documentary, poetic, realis‐ tic, efficient and so on, which are capable of reflecting an author's intention. A book on modern business practice might well be set in the crisp, no-nonsense and efficient-looking Bodoni Book, while a romantic novel might be more appro‐ priately set in the softer, more self-conscious Garamond. Only a long familiarity with types can result in a sure selection. Often a specimen setting of a page will help the designer deter‐ mine whether his choice is right.

As indicated in earlier chapters, the weaving of a book page differs with each type face. Length of line chosen to prevent doubling (reading the same line twice), proper word-spacing and line-spacing, and most of all the proper size of type in relation to the size of the page, are all important. It is essential that the designer be diverted neither by the play of texture for its own sake nor by the cold considerations of legibility alone; his task is to achieve both without the sacrifice of either. Texture is a matter of the spatial relation between words and between lines of type; legibility is a matter of the size of type in relation to the length of the line, the legibility of the type itself, and its proportion in relation to the page. The one axiom that should always apply is that the norm of legibility should be what can be read, not by a person with 20/20 vision, but by a person at the threshold of needing optical assistance.

Each text page will have a page number and a running head in most instances, although works of fiction often omit the latter. The folio should not be placed in the gutter; its function is to identify a page for the person casually flipping through the book; he must not have to dig into the binding to find it. The running head should be small and discreet, and adequately separated from the text page both by space and by the character of the type – either italics or small capitals should be used.

Normal reading practice requires the use of an indention at the beginning of a paragraph, except for the first line following a heading, or starting a new chapter. The depth of this indention will vary with the width of the type page, from an en quad on a narrow page to two or three ems on a wide page. No extra space should be inserted between paragraphs, unless there is a complete absence of an indention dictated by a designer's preference for a flush left-hand margin. Even in this case, no definition between the paragraphs is necessary unless the last line of the preceding paragraph is a full line.

No conscientious designer will permit a 'widow' to occur at the top of a page to spoil the squared corners of his page if it can possibly be avoided. But since the text is usually sacrosanct, the designer must juggle his pages in one of two ways: either varying by a line, up or down, the drop on his chapter heading, or by increasing the depth of a pair of facing pages by one line to remove the offending widow. If the bottom margin is generous enough, the reader will not notice the occasional variation from the normal margin.

While these details of refinement are important in a book, the main objective should be to invest the book with a personality. The skilled designer will do this unobtrusively but effectively. No two literary works are alike; the subject matter,

Stark black and white on a pristine white paper cover for a book of poems published by Isaacs Gallery, Toronto. This lettering by a painter, GRAHAM COUGHTRY, *caught the spirit of the poetry better than type could have done.*

the author's literary style, his philosophical approach make each book different from every other book. The fine book will reflect this difference. Those who argue that the designer's hand should not be apparent in the book overlook the fact that if a book is to have any personality, the designer's hand is bound to be evident. The very people who so argue are often designers whose good sense of typography shows through so much that the bibliophile can identify their work at once.

Personality can be achieved by the use of exotic types or luxurious paper, and some texts call for this. But the skilled designer can take a workaday type and a standard paper and, through the sheer artistry of weaving the texture of his type and placing it within the space of a page, can create a book which gives the reader a sense of aesthetic pleasure before he starts to read.

Everything that has been said about the book applies with even greater force to the typography of magazines. Consumer magazines are already reflecting new techniques for the presentation of the printed word. Books may look much the same as they did centuries ago, but few magazines look today as they did a short generation ago! In spite of that, and in spite of the fact that consumer magazines spend extravagant sums in full-colour art and photography, only the rare one shows an exciting flair of typographic ingenuity and imagination. Generally speaking the more conservative 'highbrow' magazines of literature and comment have followed dignified and impeccable typographic styles, but even some of them could well re-examine their formats and recognize the need to enrich the visual framework of their contents and to improve the typographic channels of communication for their readers.

It is in the field of the business and trade publication that new typographic approaches could be of the greatest value, and it is here where the least has been done. These publications are required reading for businessmen who wish to keep abreast

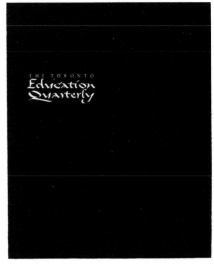

Cover and a sample article heading of a journal for teachers in Toronto, designed in 1960 by the author.

of what is new in their fields: business trends, management problems, production problems, new equipment, marketing information and trends. Yet it is a common complaint of the businessman that he never really finds time to get through all the reading he should do.

This is the fundamental problem of the editor and the typographer of the business magazine, and it has still not been properly tackled. Millions of words of technical and business information of tremendous value continue to be poured into stereotyped formats for photographs and headings, into endless columns of grey type, and thousands of businessmen spend hours of valuable executive time picking through this typographical haystack looking for the little kernels of information which pertain to them. The problem has reached the point where many businessmen, unable to cope with the sheer volume of reading matter, are taking courses to increase their reading speed. Surely this is the wrong way around. Instead of executives learning how to cover a greater acreage of stubble in order to glean a few grains of information, it should be the job of the editor to make the essential points available, and the job of the typographer to communicate them quickly.

This does not mean an indulgence in fads in type faces or tricky page layouts. It is the carrying out of a practical job of helping a busy man to pin-point the information that he needs to help him in his work. Solve this problem, and the aesthetics of presentation will come later and be relatively easy.

A business magazine, then, should be organized in such a fashion that an executive can flip through it in a matter of minutes and pick out the relevant information it contains for his further detailed reading. This is not a plea for condensed writing, or for a digest of information; it is a plea for organization of material so that a reader can see quickly the highlights of the various articles and can find those parts which concern him; he can then spend his time reading these parts thoroughly

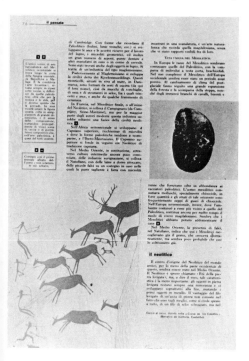

A page from the Italian technical and scientific magazine Il Leonardo *indicates how a generous outer margin to the magazine page can provide a cross-reference to the text for summary or amplification in order to speed reading.*

rather than skimming across columns of irrelevant material.

This kind of editing and typography demands more work and more attention, but surely it is more sensible for it to be done by the editor and designer rather than by the unfortunate subscriber.

Once this problem of organization is solved, the further advantage of visual stimulation can be added. The run-of-the-mill of magazines specializing in trade and business news in any one field have a sameness that is undesirable from any one publication's point of view. It would be to the publisher's interest to invest his magazine with a definite personality, a fresh look that would distinguish it from those of his com-petitors, to give it a visual verve that would make the reader welcome it as a relief from the sameness and monotony of the publications that cross his desk. If it is not economically possible to have a designer prepare each and every spread, he should be given the opportunity to create an individual, interesting format which will also provide a working, practical, formula which an editor without special design training can follow through successive issues.

Editorial pages, for instance, should break away from the restrictions imposed by the uniform 7 × 10 inch advertising page; marginal relationships can be changed; the type faces used can be up-to-date ones; areas of white space can be used for accent; pictorial material can be organized into more in-teresting groupings; fresh concepts of the link between the heading and the copy can help draw the reader to the informa-tion on the page.

These are not final answers, they are only pointers to possible areas of investigation. The aim should always be a publication which communicates faster, better, and in a stimulating man-ner. Many publications have taken tentative steps in one or the other of these directions. There is still a lot of pioneering to be done.

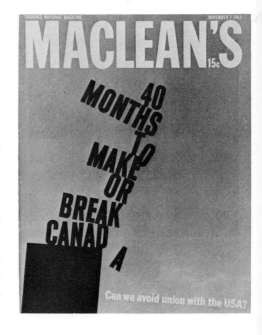

A dramatic use of type to tell a story both verbally and pictorially on a magazine cover. By ALLAN FLEMING *of Toronto.*

The history of printing, in its span of half a millennium, is the history of the impact of new schools of typographic thought on the traditional forms, and the absorption of the new ideas into the tradition. The Gutenberg Bible had only been off the press for eight years when Adolf Rusch of Strasbourg cut a 'new' type face based on humanist handwriting – the style we now call 'roman'. In 1464 this was a daring thing to do in Germany, where the black letter was the traditional letter form. Aldus Manutius of Venice, *circa* 1500, commissioned the cutting of the first italic type for his famous Aldine editions; tradition rejected the use of italic for continuous text, but retained the form for contrast or emphasis. The typographic art has never been static; the development of new styles and the revival of old ones have been part of a continuing, dynamic process. The well-informed student of the history of printing types can glance at the pages of any book and pin-point its period. Sometimes he can even identify the printer.

The last century has had more than its share of schools and movements in typography, and like fashions in clothing, the styles of the last generation can sometimes look hilariously funny – and certainly bad – to the new generation. It is only in broad historical prespective that the permanent contribution of any school can be assessed; every school adds something either directly or indirectly, as the tradition absorbs what is good in a new movement and rejects what is bad.

It is a characteristic of the movements of the last hundred years that they have followed a pattern of violent revolt against

Within the first decade after the printing of the first Bible, the German printer RUSCH *had this first roman type cut (called the fount of the R bizarre, because of its curious capital R which has been interpreted as the printer's initials – AR); German readers, used to reading the traditional black letter, must have been as shocked as people were five centuries later when* TRISTAN TZARA *designed the Dadaist announcement shown on the opposite page.*

Calligraphy in chalk on a blackboard at the Royal College of Art, London, by the man most responsible for the revival of calligraphy, EDWARD JOHNSTON.

existing forms, and out of the violent revolt has come a refining influence. Two major examples will suffice.

Victorian typography was characterized by careless type setting, blatant over-ornamentation and the indiscriminate use of a multiplicity of type faces. William Morris led the revolt by reviving the fifteenth-century page using black letterforms; the refinements of his revolt led to the revival of the beautifully even tone of the Jenson* page by the Doves Press. To this form, a movement led by Edward Johnston for the revival of calligraphy added the decorative quality of letters formed by the broad-nibbed pen. These developments took place between 1890 and 1920. This school of quiet, elegant typography was barely beginning to reform the general appearance of printing in Britain and on the continent when a new revolt occurred. A group of young artists in Zurich, the security of their world shattered by the First World War and its aftermath, rejected the dignified purity of the classic page and literally exploded the typographic page, with fragments of letters and punctuation strewn about like debris after a bombing. This was Dada and Futurist typography, and typography has never been quite the same since.

Out of the violence of this revolt came the refining influence of Jan Tschichold and his theories of dynamic typography and the asymmetric structure. His two basic books of that period, *Die neue Typografie* and *Typografische Gestaltung* are at the base of all contemporary typography; Tschichold is the acknow ledged father of all modern schools, and his work can now be seen in sufficient historical perspective for us to hazard the judgment that his name will always be associated with the liberation of the printed page from symmetry. Two other in fluences were at work with Tschichold: the Bauhaus school in Weimar, and the Dutch painter Piet Mondrian, whose com

De Evangelica, printed in a roman type by Nicolas Jenson, 1470.

positions, in their pure vertical and horizontal divisions of space, had an important effect on typographers.

Reference must also be made to the typographic schools prevailing in the 1950's and 1960's. It is, of course, impossible to assess finally the degree of influence they may have in the future, to know whether they are passing fads or whether they will become a part of the typographic tradition, but it is intriguing to speculate.

The two major schools are at opposite extremes. One called itself the 'typography of order', and was centred in Germany and Switzerland. In a sense the work of this school is an ultra-refinement of Tschichold's principles, though the master would certainly disown this offspring because of its rigid regimentation, its inhuman coldness, its mechanical dogmatism. This school builds its typographic structure on a grid of squares into which all elements must fit in definite mathematical relationships and in precise alignment. Only grotesque (sans serif) types may be used, and these in very tightly woven textures. There is a pristine crispness about the work of this school that is striking to the eye on first encounter. But the rigidity of the formula does not allow much scope for individual treatment. Solutions are predictable, and there is no concession in type style or arrangement to assist interpretation of the subject-matter. Its great advantage is that it can be taught as a set of rules; it makes no demand on creative thinking or imagination. As a result, any competent compositor can be taught the basic formula and its variations and can produce consistently well-designed pages, without having to think about the substance of the text and its interpretation.

The disadvantage is that a widespread use of the formula would diminish the individuality of printed pieces issued by various publishers or commercial firms. When all advertising or publications begin to look alike, one of the very purposes of typographic design, to impart a specific character, is defeated.

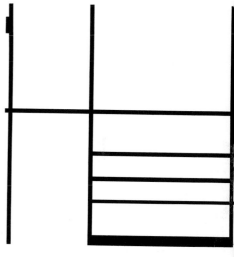

The paintings of PIET MONDRIAN *are pure examples of the plastic division of space. (Courtesy the Museum of Modern Art, New York.)*

Max Bill
Architekt BSA
Zürich

Anton Stankowski
Maler und Grafiker
Stuttgart

hans neuburg 60 jahre? als ich ihn 1930 kennenlernte, — ich machte damals das erste mal in einer fasnachtsgruppe von carigiet mit, — da waren wir doch scheinbar gleich jung? sicher täusche ich mich. er muss der ältere gewesen sein. so wenigstens kommt es heute mit· jahreszahlen ans licht.

sicher war er immer der ältere gewesen, der klügere, der über die dinge, die um ihn entstanden, schon feste ansichten hatte und diese an seine zuhörer weitergab.

ich bin der jüngere und deshalb war und ist es mir noch heute erlaubt, weniger fertige und weniger ausgereifte meinungen zu vertreten. nicht selten aber haben sich unsere ansichten gedeckt, wenn auch hin und wieder mit zeitlichem abstand.

es gibt fragen, über die wir uns immer sehr bald einig waren, nämlich fragen der qualität. über kunst und grafik hat er sich öfter als kritiker schriftlich geäussert. es wäre schön gewesen, ihm einige seiner feststellungen in einem kleinen bändchen gesammelt auf den geburtstagstisch zu legen, vor allem auch für jene, die nicht die gelegenheit hatten bis anhin hans neuburg näher zu kennen und seine urteile zu lesen.

es scheint mir, je älter hans neuburg wird, desto unabhängiger wird sein urteil und desto mutiger steht er für dieses ein. er wird mit dem älter werden jünger.
max bill

Zufall ist eine Ueberschneidung von verschiedenen Ereignissen. Aehnlich formuliert, ist eine hervorragende Persönlichkeit die Ueberschneidung verschiedener Talente und Eigenschaften. Hans Neuburg ist solch ein Schnittpunkt von sympathischen Veranlagungen. Talent, Phantasie, Intelligenz, Bildung, Beharrungsvermögen, Hilfsbereitschaft und Duldsamkeit gegenüber anders gearteten Bestrebungen zeichnen ihn aus. Ihn über eine flüchtige Bekanntschaft hinaus als Freund zu wissen, ist ein Glück, ihn als Partner bei der Arbeit zu haben, ein Gewinn.

Grafiker und Texter — so ist seine Berufsbezeichnung, ein Werbefachmann also. In diesem Beruf werden vielseitige Interessen gefordert. Diese Vielseitigkeit finden wir bei ihm nicht nur als flüchtige Orientierung, sondern Neuburg ist auf vielen Gebieten ein Anreger, Mitwirkender und Vorbild.

Mit für einen Autodidakten bemerkenswerter Weitsichtigkeit hat er sich schon Anfang der dreissiger Jahre an der Findung von Grundprinzipien innerhalb der Gebrauchsgrafik beteiligt, die heute noch Gültigkeit haben. Der kleine Kreis in Zürich mit ihm kann als eine Miniaturschule der Grafik bezeichnet werden. Carigiet, Heiniger, Eidenbenz, Lohse, Matter, Steiner, Trommer sind einige Namen der Beteiligten aus dieser Zeit. Diese Aufzählung liesse sich noch erweitern mit Namen aus dem Gebiet der Architektur, der Wirtschaft sowie der angewandten und freien Kunst. Die Eigenschaft, als Mikrobe der Entwicklung in diesen Bezirken zu wirken und überall jung zu sein, ist bis heute geblieben. Das Nachteilige an Neuburg ist für mich,

dass er seinen Wohnsitz in Zürich und nicht in Stuttgart hat.
Anton Stankowski

Some qualities of the typography of order will doubtless survive and have their influence in applications where rigidity is an asset. Other influences are impinging upon the technique and acting to humanize it, retaining its orderliness, but without extreme regimentation. But certainly if all printed matter were to fall into the present pattern of this school it would be a monotonous and dreary typographic world indeed.

At the other extreme is a school which has no name except those applied to it by its detractors: the typography of disorder, or 'beatnik' typography. This is a scissors-and-paste-pot school of typography which has resulted from a number of technological developments.

The first of these is the extensive use today of the offset lithographic process in the printing industry. (This process does not print directly from metal types but uses a photographic method.) Parallel with that is the development of various forms of photo-typesetting and the availability to printers of letters in adhesive-backed sheets. These new techniques make it possible for the artist to become his own compositor and make-up man, bypassing both type composition and photo-engraving. Instead of being subjected to the discipline of rectangular metal types assembled in a composing stick, and to the pressman's chase, he is completely at liberty to cut up and stick down letters without inhibition. He can tuck them in together, jumble them, mix sizes and styles, put them inside each other, twist them, run them at angles. He is not troubled by the 'shoulder' of types because they do not exist on his proofs; therefore he can pile his letters one on top of the other.

This school is essentially Dadaism with even the technical restrictions removed. Naturally such freedom can lead to abuse in the hands of the undisciplined and those without sound knowledge of printing and typographic techniques and of principles of design. But even the wildest concoctions contain

dem interesse und verständnis unserer kundschaft ihrer geduld hilfsbereitschaft und begeisterung für das was die musik uns allen schönes bringt ist es zu danken dass die weihnachtssaison in basels erstem geschäft für grammophonplatten für alle beteiligten erfreulich und erfolgreich war wir haben viele neue freunde gewonnen und hoffen sie zu erhalten und noch weitere zu gewinnen dank kompetentem service und einem lager das unsern wahlspruch wahr macht: alle platten bei derrik olsen im shopping center drachen basel

telephon 23 04 23

boîte à musique

On the opposite page is an example of the format of the 'Swiss school' as it appeared in a booklet on Hans Neuburg, one of the originators of the style. It was designed by his colleague on the magazine Graphic Design, CARLO VIVARELLI *of Zurich. Both the merits and defects of the style are apparent in this page. Above is an example of an advertisement in which greater liberty is taken with the format without losing the clean-cut quality. Designed by* GERSTNER+KUTTER *of Basle.*

Scissors and paste-pot typography— an example from Saint Mary's College, Notre Dame, Indiana, under the supervision of SISTER MARIE ROSAIRE, C.S.C., *and* NORMAN LALIBERTÉ.

Two examples of highly organized massing of cut letters to create textural impact; above, by THEO DIMSON, *Toronto, and below, by* WALTER SCHILLER, *Leipzig.*

the seeds of new forms of typographic expression; certainly what is being accomplished is a legitimate exploitation of the freedom conferred by the offset process and the fact that letterforms are liberated from the rectangular prisons of composing-room practice. Even the lack of knowledge of the technical aspects of typography can lead these designers to approach letterforms and their combinations with fresh vision. The task of refining the discoveries of this school of disorder awaits some new Tschichold who can seize on what is lasting in it and make it a part of the tradition of typographic communication.

These two schools stand at the far extremes of typographic development in this period, but there are a number of important trends, based on much less sweeping innovations, which may also have their influence on the typography of the future. The principal one uses the camera as one of the tools of the typographer. In many cases the designer becomes his own photographer, capable of achieving the exact result he wants. In other cases the photographer is an associate working under the designer's instruction, or the designer simply has access to a wide range of photographic source-material and uses it. This new approach can be traced to the specialization which is characteristic of our times. The day when the typographer and the illustrator were one is almost past; most typographic designers today are that and no more; their ability as draughtsmen, if they have any at all, is indifferent. To this modern designer, the camera becomes a substitute for his lack of drawing ability; it makes him the composite illustrator-typographer. And because he is still primarily a designer of print, he approaches the camera in a new way, just as the artist approaches type in a new way when he is technically incompetent to handle metal type itself.

This new combination, where the lead, tin, and antimony of type metal are combined, figuratively speaking, with the silver

Photographic distortion of type by
FRANCO GRIGNANI *of Milan in this advertisement for a*
printing firm goes beyond the bounds of legibility,
but piques the curiosity of the reader.

nitrate of the photographic process, has precipitated some new approaches that are not important enough to be classified as schools, yet are sufficiently vigorous and imaginative to have tremendous future potential. A number of combinations are being used, and they deserve brief mention here.

The rebus is occasionally employed as a method of typo graphic presentation. In it a word which is part of a larger word is treated photographically. A striking example was the use of the word 'hearing' in a brochure for CBS: the letters 'ear' were dropped and an embossed representation of a human ear was substituted.

Photographs can be used as substitutes for letters, where their shapes resemble those of the letters and where they do not impede recognition of the word. Perhaps the first use of this technique was by Jean Carlu in a famous poster urging greater production in the early years of World War II. The 'o' of 'production' became a nut which was being tightened by a wrench held in a gloved hand.

Photographs of products or situations are often cut out in the shape of one or more letters; sometimes the photograph is continuous through the word, and unifies the word so that picture and word are one. Photographs can also be inserted into large letters, or become the terminal points of interroga tory or exclamatory punctuation. An alternative is to put the photograph inside the letter, filling the counter or counters of the letter form.

Typographers manipulate letter forms through photographic processes to create distortions and movement which challenge the eye and pique the curiosity of the reader.

These are all specific instances of the complete integration of the photograph with typographic letters. It is, of course, common usage to employ the photograph as an independent area standing in distinct relationship to the area of a type mass, but in these newer forms, the photograph is one of the integral elements of the word image, and all the rules of typographic concord and contrast apply just as though the photograph were a type element. When using photographic techniques the typo graphic designer often likes to avoid the rather sterile 8 × 10 inch proportion in favour of tall, thin verticals, long, narrow horizontals, or perfect squares. With his own camera slung over his shoulder he often 'designs' his photographic layout in the viewfinder.

Many levels of contrast occur in this title spread of a book designed by PAT GANGNON *of Toronto, not the least of which is found in the shapes of the photographs.*

Typographers are still probing the discovery made by Dr W. J. H. Sandberg of Holland that the inner forms of letters – their counters – have shapes as interesting as the letters them selves. In his little book *Experimenta Typographica,* Sandberg projects this to his reader:

The unusual forms of the middle line are the inner forms of the letters and the spaces between the letters; the background has become the form and the letters are now the background. This experiment has had a number of applications, primarily one in which the letters are reversed against a ground, and other colours are introduced in the counters of the letters. The letters are white forms, but the counters, usually multicoloured, become a new element interwoven between the letter and the ground, and relating first to one and then to the other.

Typographical word-play has become a sort of designer's game to amuse the public into accepting the message. It indi cates the unsuspected presence of a sense of humour in the too serious business of communication. The game simply consists of treating the word typographically in such a way that the word contains its own illustration. A number of examples are

per.od

com,ma

c:l:n

addding

subtrcting

multimultiplying

div id ing

NON-CONFORMISt

A group of typographical 'puns' from a tiny booklet, 'Watching Words Move', by CHERMAYEFF & GEISMAR, *New York, is shown above. At right, an experiment by* TERRY PRITCHETT *done at the University of Iowa.*

dri_p

dro_p

dri_p

dro_p

dri_p

dro_p

shown to indicate the range of this word-play; but the viewer will be aware that this game is a more sophisticated extension of the trite treatment of the word 'LOOK' in which the two o's are made to look like eyes.

Resembling this game, but not involving words, is the use of single typographic elements, with or without a photographic or illustrative accompaniment, to convey a wordless message. A typical example of this technique is the substitution for the words 'NO SMOKING' of a cigarette and an X grouped into a single pattern.

Finally, no discussion of new typographic forms would be complete without some reference to and examples of typography in motion, as seen in film and television. The motion picture industry had long been satisfied to flash inanimate titles and credits across the screen like so many still slides. Two events made typographers in this field realize that typography could be more effective when use was made of the motion inherent in the medium. The first was the production of a series of abstract films by Norman McLaren of Canada's National Film Board. The highly original antics and activities of lines, dots, loops, numbers, and other shapes across the screen became a jumping-off point for typographic designers who began to see letters as active instead of static elements.

The second event was the growth of the television industry and the need for more and more originality in station identification and programme titling on the one hand and in sponsors' messages on the other. The full potential of the television screen cannot be achieved by using it only to project a series of showcard messages, and advertisers realized this. One might just as well place these messages in newspapers where at least they can remain within view instead of disappearing after a brief exposure, and where they may even be given subsequent exposure. Television, in its use of filmed commercials, offered the possibility of typography animated to put the message

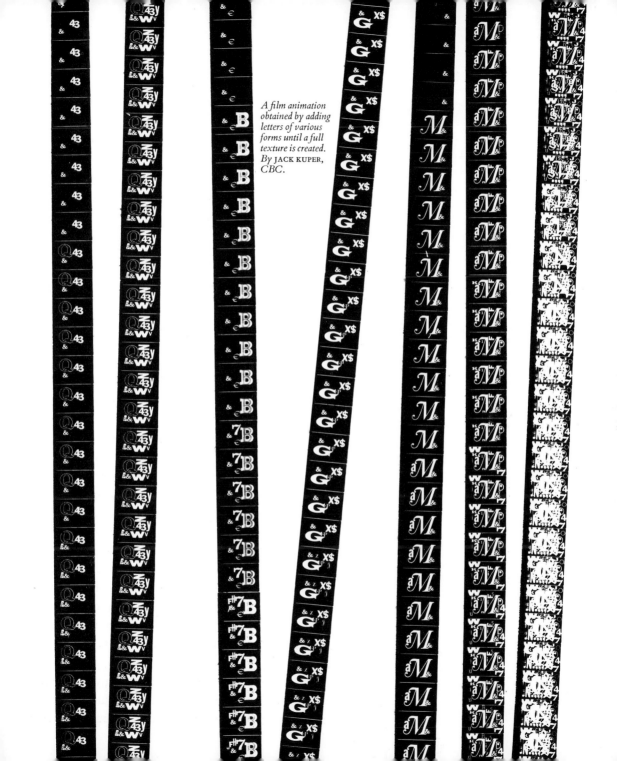

A film animation obtained by adding letters of various forms until a full texture is created. By JACK KUPER, CBC.

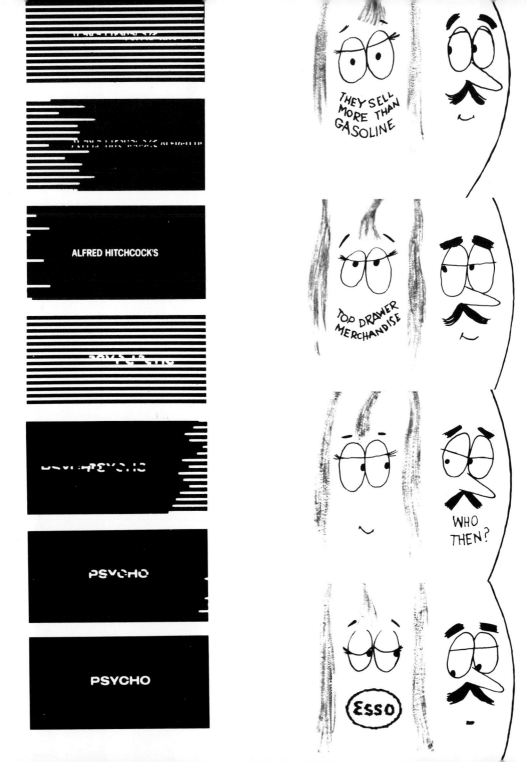

across in a lively, entertaining, and more memorable fashion. McLaren's films such as *Dots and Loops, Begone Dull Care,* and *Rhythmetic,* had already explored what might be done with the animation of abstract forms, letters, figures, and words. Graphic artists at the Canadian Broadcasting Corporation, led by David MacKay, also tackled titling problems with imagination and humour and won international plaudits for their work. In doing so they pioneered new forms which will eventually influence film and television titling and television commercials throughout the world. The possibilities have only begun to be explored but the breakthrough in concept from still typography to typography in motion has taken place.

The movie industry was not slow to see the graphic possibilities in the animation of titles, and Saul Bass of California contributed some highly original titles. It is unfortunate that there is no way to put a sample of typographic animation permanently into a book of this nature. Simply to show a series of stills of different stages of the animation takes typography back to the very thing from which it has liberated itself. In spite of this difficulty, the reproduction of single frames from Saul Bass's titles for the movie *Psycho* can be instructive. The horizontal lines illustrated opposite moved in and out across the screen, until certain lines with their broken edges became synchronized, the broken edges met to form letters, and typographic word patterns emerged. This is only one of a number of stimulating techniques which Saul Bass has introduced to Hollywood.

The whole field of typographic movement presents a challenge to the experimenter and a rich market for the successful innovator. The creative designer of animated messages has to leave behind him the static concepts of the printed page and think in time as well as in space. A whole new set of concepts must be developed to deal with three-dimensional effects, too, for the camera is capable of creating strong three-dimensional

Opposite page: single frames from the title for Psycho *by* SAUL BASS, *as described on this page. At right, frames from a television commercial for* Esso *designed by* CLIFF ROBERTS; *the words come in as 'voice over', while the visual words replace the mouths of the character during dialogue.*

A circular movement of type appropriate to the title by WIM CROUWEL *of Amsterdam.*

Opposite page: movement of simple geometric elements on the painting surface has been a rich shaft of experimentation and invention for VICTOR VASARELY *of France, and offers a challenge to typographic designers.*

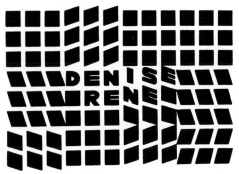

French painter VICTOR VASARELY *employs his surface movement to create a commercial message for the Galerie Denise Renée, in the upper example; below,* ALDO CALABRESI *of Milan adapts it to a vigorous pharmaceutical advertisement.*

illusions in a two-dimensional plane by presenting the motion of objects through a background and in relation to each other, giving a powerful effect of spatial depth. Typographic communication on the television or movie screen can become a true ballet of communication in the hands of a typographic choreographer.

It was inevitable that typographers working on the static, two-dimensional surface of the printed page should be affected by the visual kinetics of cinematic typography. A group of French painters calling itself '*le mouvement*' has already experimented with the creation of the sense of movement on a surface. The work of Victor Vasarely is of special interest here. The study of typography in motion has been a jumping-off point for a few experimenters who have simultaneously become intrigued with the patterns associated with computers and other electronic devices.

At the present time no clear school of typography has emerged from this play with pattern and movement; a school may indeed never emerge, but certainly the experimentation will have side effects. The area where it may have its greatest impact and achieve its greatest development could well be in the mushrooming graphic arts industries in developing countries. Craftsmen and designers, unhampered by a tradition of literacy which teaches people to look at words in sequence, one after another,* are exploiting with a fresh viewpoint the new film and electronic techniques that are revolutionizing the printing industry. They may very well be the progenitors of a new typography.

The embryonic forms of this new, non-lineal approach are evident to anyone who has had the stimulating experience of

*Those who wish to pursue this complex subject of the impact of the new electronic means of communication on societies with and without literate backgrounds should read *The Gutenberg Galaxy* and *Understanding Media* by Marshall McLuhan.

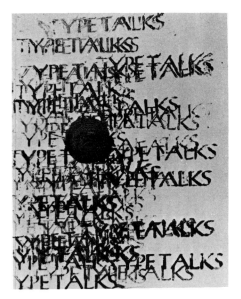

A layout by a Jamaican student for a magazine cover: an indication of the direction that designers in emerging countries may take toward low definition but high participation in their design.

teaching typographic design to students from a society where there is no long tradition of literacy. Too strict a discipline, of course, will stifle natural expression in the student; a sincere teacher will understand that only techniques and basic design principles can be taught, and that from there on the emerging societies must find the form of graphic communication best suited to their own concepts and traditions; the results will not be, as they should not be, facsimiles of the products of literate communities.

This 'new typography' will probably outrage European and North American designers, whether they work with traditional or *avant garde* forms; but for three-quarters of the world's people it will be the dominant typographic form of communication as we move into the twenty-first century. It will be a part of their intellectual, social and spiritual liberation, as vital for them as Gutenberg's invention of movable type has been for Europe from the fifteenth century on.

Finally, we are on the verge of new developments which may well affect the nature of our alphabet. The twin needs of a letterform which can be read by electronic scanning devices, and a new *scripta franca* which will be non-phonetic so that, like numerals, it can be read regardless of language, may well result in a new communication form. The writer believes that the system devised by Louis Braille in 1825 for teaching the blind to read offers the greatest possibilities, once its phonetic basis is abandoned. This six-position domino grid offers 720 potential combinations; if this grid is surrounded by other three-position grids to act as determinants, tense indicators, etc., the potential combinations reach over 20,000 words. For the purposes of storage of information in computer memory banks, a straight 9-position grid offers over 360,000 combinations; the feed-back in this form would make any stored data available for decoding instantly, without translation, into any spoken language.

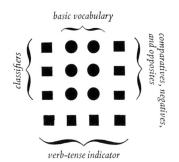

basic vocabulary

classifiers

comparatives, negatives, and opposites

verb–tense indicator

epilogue

Four major developments have come to the writer's attention over the past year in the course of performing jury duty for several exhibitions, or through the helpfulness of fellow designers in drawing attention to them. Curiously, all of them have taken place in the field of literature and book publishing; one might be led to infer that commercial advertising is now becoming a conservative force, preferring to stick to what is safe, while the book, once tightly hedged in by strict observance of the rules of legibility, is becoming a fertile field for experimentation.

Silence, by John Cage, was perhaps the first major break. It represents the collaboration of a skilled typographer, Raymond Grimaila, and a musical composer and lecturer, Mr Cage. In this book, a number of different forms of typographic presentation are used, but all of them are based on the author's desire to achieve the typographical equivalent of musical rhythm and structure, and in some cases to let *into* the typographic page the open space which is characteristic of the sculpture of Henry Moore, and of Mr Cage's own compositions.

For over a decade, the development of concrete poetry has shown promise of opening up new avenues of thought for typographic designers. The high point of this movement was the exhibition 'Between Poetry and Painting' held at the end of 1965 at the Institute of Contemporary Arts in London, England, and subsequently shown on the continent. Some examples that appeared there are reproduced here. The reader should also include in this group the composition by Diter Rot on page 20.

Specimen page from Silence, *designed by composer* JOHN CAGE *and* RAYMOND GRIMAILA, *Wesleyan University Press.*

Here we are now			at the middle
	of the fourth large part		of this talk.
More and more		I have the feeling	that we are getting
nowhere.	Slowly	,	as the talk goes on
,	we are getting	nowhere	and that is a pleasure
.	It is not irritating	to be where one is	. It is
only irritating	to think one would like	to be somewhere else.	Here we are now
,	a little bit after the	middle	of the
fourth large part		of this talk	.
	More and more	we have the feeling	
	that I am getting	nowhere	
	Slowly	,	as the talk goes on
		¶	
,	slowly	,	we have the feeling
	we are getting	nowhere.	That is a pleasure
	which will continue	.	If we are irritated
,	it is not a pleasure	.	Nothing is not a
pleasure	if one is irritated	.	but suddenly
,	it is a pleasure	,	and then more and more
	it is not irritating	.	(and then more and more
	and slowly	).	Originally
	we were nowhere	;	and now, again
	we are having	the pleasure	
,	slowly	nowhere.	If anybody
of being	,	let him go to sleep	.
is sleepy		¶	
Here we are now			at the beginning of the
ninth unit	of the fourth large part		of this talk.
More and more		I have the feeling	that we are getting
nowhere.	Slowly	,	as the talk goes on
,	we are getting	nowhere	and that is a pleasure
.	It is not irritating	to be where one is	. It is
only irritating	to think one would like	to be somewhere else.	Here we are now
,	a little bit after the	beginning	of the ninth unit of the
fourth large part		of this talk	.
	More and more	we have the feeling	

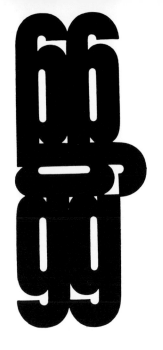

The full development of this form emerged from the work of a group of poets in Brazil working in the academic field of communication theory; their manifesto of 1964 established the premise: 'Language is any set of signs plus the way they are used – i.e., the way they are related to each other (syntax), provided with referents (semantics), and interpreted (pragmatics).' The material reproduced will indicate what a rich and stimulating field of typographic source material this new literary form can provide.

Examples of concrete poetry from an exhibition at the Institute of Contemporary Art:
HANSJÖRG MAYER, *Germany*
PEDRO XISTO, *Brazil*
HENRI CHOPIN, *Paris*

EPITHALAMIUM - II

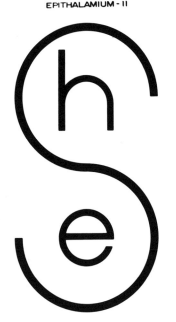

he & she
or
s - serpens
h - homo
e - eva

LE POEME ALPHABETIQUE

réalisé 20 siècles après J.-C., soit après une très longue réflexion

aaaaaaaaaaaaaaaaaaaaaaaaaaaaaaaaaaaaaaaaaaaaaaaaaaaaaaaaa
bbbbbbbbbbbbbbbbbbbbbbbbbbbbbbbbbbbbbbbbbbbbbbbbbbbbbbbbbb
ccccccccccccccccccccccccccccccccccccccccccccccccccccccccccc
ddddddddddddddddddddddddddddd dddddddddddddddddddddddddddd
eeeeeeeeee eeeeeeeeeeeeeeeeeee eeeeeeeeeeeeeeeeeeeeeeeeee
ffffffffff ffffffffffffffffffffff fffffffffff ffffffffff
gggggggg gggggggggggggggggggggggg gggggggggg gggggggggg
hhhhhhh hhhhhhhhhhhhhhhhhhhhhhhhh hhhhhhh hhhhhhhhhhhh
iiiiii iiiiiiiiiiiiiiiiiiiiiiiiiii iiiii iiiiiiiiiiii
jjjjj jjjjjjjjjjjjjjjjjjjjjjjjjjjjj jjj jjjjjjjjjjjjj
kkkk kkkkkkkkkkkkkkkkkkkkkkkkkkkk k kkkkkkkkkkkkkkk
111 11111111111111111111111111111111 11111111111111111
mmmmmmmmmmmmmmmmmmmmmmmmmmmmmmmmmmmmmmmm mmmmmmmmmmmmmmmmmm
nnnnnnnnnnnnnnnnnnnnnnnnnnnnnnnnnnnnnnnn nnnnnnnnnnnnnn
ooooo ooooooooo ooooooooooooooooooooooo oooooooooo
oooo ooooooooooo ooooooooooooooooooooooo oooooooooo
ppp ppppppppppppp pppppppppppppppppppppp pppppppppp
qqqqqqqqqqqqqqqqqq qqqqqqqqqqqqqqqqqqqqqqq qqqqqqqq
rrrrrrrrrrrrrrrrrrr rrrrrrrrrrrrrrrrrrrrrrrr rrrrrrrr
sssssssssssssssssssss sssssssssssssssssssssss ssssssss
ttttttttttttttttttttt tttttttt ttttttttttttttttt tttttt
uuuuuuuuuuuuuuuuuuuuuu uuuuuu uuuuuuuuuuuuuuuuu uuuuu
vvvvvvvvvvvvvvvvvvvvvv vvvv vvvvvvvvvvvvvvvvv vvvv
wwwwwwwwwwwwwwwwwwwwww ww wwwwwwwwwwwwwwwwwww www
xxxxxxxxxxxxxxxxxxxxxxx x xxxxxxxxxxxxxxxxxxxx xxxx
xxxxxzzzzzzzzzzzzzzzzzzzzzzzzzzzzzzzzzzzzzzzzzzzzzzzz zzzz

abcdefghijklmnopqrstuvwxz

il manque toujours l'y

yyyyyyyyyyyyyyyyyyyyyyyyyyyyyyyyyyyyyyyyyyyyyyyyyyyyyyyy
q u e l l e   i m p o r t a n c e

The Czech typographer Oldřich Hlavsa is well known beyond the borders of his country for his bold experimentation with letters, particularly his typographic covers for the Czech trade magazine *Typografia* (see page 24). In 1965 he designed for a Czechoslovakian poetry book club an edition devoted to the poems of Guillaume Apollinaire. Every page of text throughout this book is an imaginative typographic interpretation, a treatment of which Apollinaire would certainly have approved, a fitting complement to the poet's own calligrams.

VATU V UŠÍCH — — — — — — — — — — — — — —

Tolik třaskavin na jeden jediný **CÍL!**

Napiš   *Prů*
slovo   *střely*
troufáš-   *v*
li-si   *mé*
                       duši
                       věčně   *Tvé*
?   *roz*   *dravé*
                       vál   *stádo*
                       čené   *chrlí*
                                              oheň

OMEGAFON

Kdo smrti unikal až dosud
ten čekal jenom na jinou
co přišlo od severu odsud
pokrylo slunce samou tmou
Co chcete   *je to jeho osud*

VZHŮRU   MAZÁCI

In the summer of 1965, a distinguished international jury awarded a gold medal of the International Book Exhibition at Leipzig to an edition of the play, *La Cantatrice Chauve** by Eugène Ionesco, published by Editions Gallimard in Paris and designed by the French typographer, Massin. Among the thou 1 sands of magnificent books submitted to this exhibition, this volume represented a radical departure from the typographic conventions of the book and earned the unanimous approval of judges of diverse viewpoints, social philosophies, and cul 1 tural backgrounds. The few illustrations here can only give a fragmentary view of the way in which the designer in effect brings the stage play to the reader; one does not really *read* this book, one attends a performance typographically staged by Massin with the collaboration of the photographer Henry Cohen. Here are the inflections of voice, the awkward silences, the hubbub of multiple voices, the restrained speech, and the shouted epithet, all given visual form through typography.

These are the first rumblings of change. He would be a brave man who would attempt to answer the obvious question:

Quo vadimus?

* *The Bald Soprano*, an identical edition in English, has been published by The Grove Press, New York.

Spread from La Cantatrice Chauve *by*
Eugène Ionesco, published by Editions Gallimard,
Paris, and designed by MASSIN.

Spread from La Cantatrice Chauve *by Eugène Ionesco, published by Editions Gallimard, Paris, and designed by* MASSIN.

Spread from La Cantatrice Chauve *by*
Eugène Ionesco, published by Editions Gallimard,
Paris, and designed by MASSIN.

bibliography

The acquisition of a typographic library is the work of a lifetime, and the books chosen will reflect the specific interests of the collector. This bibliography is only intended to answer the question, so often asked by students, 'What books should I buy to help me?' The list appended here can be purchased for around $100.

This is the definitive historical work on which any typographic library should be built:

PRINTING TYPES: THEIR HISTORY, FORMS & USE
    by D. B. Updike;
    2nd edition, published by HARVARD UNIVERSITY PRESS,
    Cambridge, 1937; 2 volumes, profusely illustrated.

One of the following should augment a collection of typefounder's specimen sheets:

TREASURY OF ALPHABETS AND LETTERING
    by Jan Tschichold;
    published by REINHOLD PUBLISHING CORP., New York, 1966;
    240 pages with 176 plates.

A BOOK OF TYPE AND DESIGN by Oldřich Hlavsa;
    published by TUDOR PUBLISHING CO., New York, 1960;
    495 pages, profusely illustrated.

Book designers would be wise to secure both of the following:

DESIGNING BOOKS by Jan Tschichold;
    published by WITTENBORN, SCHULTZ, INC., New York.

AN INTRODUCTION TO TYPOGRAPHY by Oliver Simon;
    2nd edition, published by FABER & FABER, London, 1963;
    137 pages, many specimens and illustrations.
    (Also available in a Penguin paperback edition.)

Those interested in the broader principles of design, and teachers of graphic design, will find these books indispensable:

LANGUAGE OF VISION by Gyorgy Kepes;
    published by PAUL THEOBALD, Chicago, 1945;
    224 pages, 318 illustrations.

GRAPHIC DESIGN MANUAL by Armin Hofman;
    published by REINHOLD PUBLISHING CORP., New York, 1965;
    172 pages, almost entirely illustrated.

*For a comprehensive survey of mechanical methods of typesetting
and reproduction methods:*

ATA HANDBOOK OF ADVERTISING PRODUCTION
    by Leonard F. Bahr;
    published by the ADVERTISING TYPOGRAPHERS OF AMERICA, INC.,
    461 Eighth Avenue, New York 1; 1954.

*Advertising and editorial designers concerned with contemporary
typographic refinements should have:*

TYPOGRAPHY by Aaron Burns;
    published by REINHOLD PUBLISHING CORP., New York, 1961;
    112 pages, 130 illustrations.

*For a comprehensive study of typographic design, the specimens of
twentieth-century typography selected for the first international
exhibition of typography under the sponsorship of The International
Center for the Typographic Arts, Inc. is invaluable:*

TYPOMUNDUS 20;
    published by REINHOLD PUBLISHING CORP.; 224 pages
    550 specimens.

*Teachers of graphic design should ask their school library
to make available:*

THE THINKING EYE by Paul Klee;
    published by LUND HUMPHRIES, London, and GEORGE WITTENBORN,
    INC., New York, 1961; 540 pages, 188 halftone illustrations
    and 1183 of the artist's line drawings.

visuell tractat

appendix

containing reproductions

of a number of pertinent specimens

which have either been

too recently acquired

to find their proper place in the text,

or were considered too important

to be confined to the marginal space.

Opposite: cover of booklet for Gruppe 56, Germany; the black was printed on the paper cover, and the red on a tissue overwrap. The black has been screened here in an attempt to recreate the effect. Designed by H. W. KAPITSKI.

This page: Calligraphy by MARIA VIANI, *courtesy* CUAS, *publication of The Cooper Union Art School, New York.*

156: Experimental page emphasizing character of the individual letter by TERRY PRITCHETT, *University of Iowa.*

157: Interruption of rhythm demonstrated by LEO LIONNI *for Fortune Magazine.*

158: Experiments with creating motion and interrupting it by ANTON STANKOWSKI *of Stuttgart.*

159: Poster for a design exhibition by the NIPPON DESIGN CENTRE, *Tokyo.*

160: A few specimens of alphabetic patterns created by two or more printings at different angles, from a limited edition by KURT H. VOLK, *New York.*

161: A typographic composition of strong inscriptional quality by HERMANN ZAPF, *Frankfurt am Main. (From Manuale Typographicum by Hermann Zapf, Museum Books, New York.)*

162: The cover of one of a series of booklets on typography published by Westvaco, New York, has a figure as its dominant design motif. Designed by the author.

163: This page from a booklet Petit Testament d'un Typographe by MAXIMILIEN VOX *of France established the cadence of the poem by the use of changes in the word spacing, while maintaining extra tight line spacing.*

"Each letter of the alphabet constitutes in itself a self-contained element of book design. Its contours, proportions, the distribution of negative spaces, the shape of its positive areas contribute to the visual tensions which are necessary to give a form an expression. These properties become more evident when a letter is enlarged beyond 'normal' size and thus are exposed as an individual design. A single letter can become a bold & welcome medium of typographic planning."
Herbert Bayer

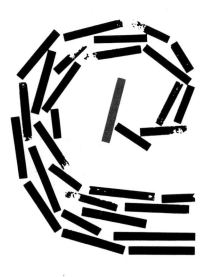

日本のデザイン展望

83デザイン・イヤー参加展

日

exhibition
designs
today

5月10日〜15日／協賛 世界デザイン会議
渋谷 東横 新館7階催物場

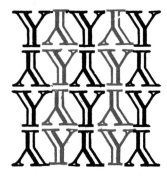

Das Größeste ist das Alphabet, ABC *denn alle Weisheit steckt darin.* DEF
GHIJKLMNOP
Aber nur der erkennt den Sinn, QRST *der's recht zusammen- zusetzen versteht.*
UVWXY&Z

E. GEIBEL

A TYPOGRAPHIC QUEST NUMBER FOUR

the
organization
of space

WESTVACO

Quand je mourrai   typos de France
plantez un cyprès sur ma tombe
mieux que le vert de l'espérance
sur l'arbre noir   le blanc-colombe

LE TYPOGRAPHE

COLOPHON

The text of this book was typeset at the University of Toronto Press in 11-point Monotype Bembo, with 3-point leading. The chapter headings are in 14-point Linotype Helvetica. The printing was done by offset lithography by Edwards Brothers in Ann Arbor, Michigan, and the paper is 80# Westvaco Coronation Litho Dull. The book is bound in Linson cloth printed by offset lithography.